Let's Make Love

Let's Make Love

THE MEANING OF SEXUAL INTERCOURSE

JACK DOMINIAN

DARTON·LONGMAN + TODD

This book is dedicated to students,
their parents and teachers.

First published in 2001 by
Darton, Longman and Todd Ltd
1 Spencer Court
140–142 Wandsworth High Street
London SW18 4JJ

ISBN 0–232–52338–X

A catalogue record for this book is available from the British Library.

Designed by Sandie Boccacci
Phototypeset in 9.5/13pt Utopia by Intype London Ltd
Printed and bound in Great Britain by
Page Bros, Norwich

Contents

Contents

IV. Challenges for the Contemporary Church

Preface

This book was written because the twentieth century saw the end of a tradition, spanning 20 centuries, that linked sexuality with procreation. In one way or another this tradition seemed suspicious of sexual pleasure and safeguarded sex by linking it with new life. With the advent of contraception and a much wider understanding of the meaning of sex, that era has come to an end.

It is my opinion that this has left a vacuum that neither society nor the Churches have been able to fill adequately. The Churches have advanced from linking sex with procreation to linking it with love, but since sexual love is an extremely difficult concept to understand and appreciate, with a few exceptions, the Churches are sidestepping the task of exploring sexual love. Instead, they are obsessed with homosexuality in the Protestant tradition and with contraception in the Roman Catholic one. I consider this response a serious breach of responsibility by the Churches to their people and to the community as a whole. I believe society is hungry for a serious dialogue about sexual love, which I have tried to provide in this book.

How the contents will be received is up to you, the reader, but the failure of the Churches to prepare their people for the move from seeing sex as a means of procreation to sex as a means of expressing love, has meant that society and the people of God have taken matters into their own hands and are experimenting widely. For some conservatives in all the Christian Churches, this experimentation is regarded with shock and horror. Personally, I believe that a radical transformation in the way we see sexuality is necessary and I do not hesitate to say so.

I believe that, while the step from biology to love is the right one, the implications of the sexual revolution are monumental and so far the Churches have only scratched the surface. I am well aware that one person and one book cannot provide all the answers, but it is my invitation to move from the statement, 'In the beginning was the word and the word was "No"' to an 'Amen' that sees the divine image in sex and the erotic.

I do not tackle such issues as abortion, homosexuality, masturbation, marital breakdown and divorce, because they have been dealt with extensively elsewhere and because my primary objective has been to describe the ordinary, everyday experience of sexual intercourse in extraordinary divine terms.

I believe the sexual revolution has opened the horizons of sexuality, but society has not taken the opportunity seriously and has trivialised sex. I believe the Churches have an opportunity to show to the world that, if God is to be taken seriously – and there is massive evidence that men and women want to do this – then one way of doing this is to recognise the presence of the divine in the sexual, interpersonal encounter between people.

The Christian tradition in this area, with very few exceptions, is deeply flawed and I begin the book with five historical chapters tracing this tradition from the Old and New Testaments, through the patristic and medieval periods to the Reformation and the twentieth century. What is conspicuous and amazing is that, until the last 30 to 40 years, mention of love was on the whole absent. Instead, what those centuries established was the importance of the single state dedicated to God, the celibate clergy, the link between sex and procreation, and the fear of pleasure. It is an enormous task to retrace our steps to see that God is love, all creation is related to love, and sex expresses it most powerfully.

Having finally in the last few decades made the link between sex, relationship and love, Part II opens with an outline of the physical and psychological basis of sex. It then moves to the heart of the book which is a detailed examination of love in sexual intercourse. As far as I know this has never been done before in this way. I examine attraction, the personal, interpersonal, procreative and moral aspects of coitus (and also sexual difficulties), the heart of the mystery of sexual intercourse and link it with love. If we are to understand the shift from biology to love, these chapters are crucial to the theme of this book.

In Part III I deal with descriptions of coitus in unusual situations, teenage intercourse, cohabitation, adultery and the moral implications of these patterns. Youthful intercourse is the result of earlier sexual maturation and cohabitation of the long gap between puberty and marriage. These are new arrivals on the scene and have their own specific moralities. In particular, cohabitation needs an historic understanding of marriage to make sense of it. There is nothing new in adultery, and disapproval of it remains as strong as ever.

Prostitution and pornography are perennial situations – the latter much accelerated – which see sex impersonally. In Christian terms, these are the heresies of sexuality. My answer to these two problems is not to actively suppress them, but to positively enhance loving sexuality, so that both prostitutes and pornography become increasingly unnecessary.

Although, as with all my books, this one is addressed to the Christian community as a whole, in Part IV I devote three chapters to specific Roman Catholic issues. I analyse the mistakes of *Humanae Vitae* in detail, urge a voluntary celibacy of the clergy and, applying it beyond the Catholic community, the desirability of a single state dedicated to God.

This book will undoubtedly receive a mixed reception. For many it will fulfil long-awaited expectations. For a minority it will be disturbing. This anxiety has been anticipated in letters I have received over the years. The number of objections have been minute compared to the approval and encouragement, but in the last part of the book I wanted to answer, if not to satisfy, my critics.

I devote a single chapter to evangelisation which I consider of vital importance. Briefly, my case is that the Christian Churches are haemorrhaging. This is for a variety of reasons but one of them, particularly for the young, is the attitude to sexuality. I finish the book with the blunt assertion that Christianity must face the challenge of the sexual revolution and evaluate it. On the positive side, the sexual revolution has liberated and made welcome the wonder of sex. On the negative side, it has trivialised it. This book is a challenge to Christianity not to be held back by fear, but to look at revelation as the answer through love to the fullness of sex, and a challenge to be wary of tradition for it is flawed and yet to discern what is good in it. I am committed to the view that we should be grateful to the secular world for its contribution to our understanding of sexuality. Now it is up to Christianity, through revelation, to realise the wonder of sex as the image of the divine in men and women.

Part I

A Brief History
of Christianity and Sex

Chapter 1

The Judeo-Christian Background

This book is dedicated to the history and meaning of sexual intercourse. It traces the origin from the Hebrew tradition in Genesis and brings it up to date in our contemporary period. It is a study which reflects the vicissitudes or changes of circumstances of sexuality and summarises how one religious tradition has treated this most intimate of personal subjects. The story begins with the two accounts in Genesis. The second is the older of the two, traditionally know as the Yahwistic, and dates from about the tenth century BC.

Yahweh God said, 'It is not right that man should be alone. I shall make him a helper.' So from the soil Yahweh God fashioned all the wild beasts and all the birds of heaven. These he brought to the man to see what he would call them; each one was to bear the name the man would give it. The man gave names to all the cattle, all the birds of heaven and all the wild animals. But no helper suitable for man was found for him. So Yahweh God made the man fall into a deep sleep. And while he slept, he took one of his ribs and enclosed it in flesh. Yahweh God built the rib he had taken from the man into a woman and brought her to the man. The man exclaimed:

This at last is bone from my bones,
And flesh from my flesh!
This is to be called woman,
For this was taken from man.

This is why a man leaves his father and mother and joins himself to his wife, and they become one body.

Now both of them were naked, the man and his wife, but they felt no shame before each other. (Gen. 2:18–25)

In the most comprehensive, theological commentary on the body,[1] John Paul II uses the two passages in Genesis – particularly the one above – to proclaim the physical, social and spiritual equality of the sexes. The woman is intrinsically related to the man in that it was one of his ribs that formed the basis of her creation.

He goes on to describe in detail the created readiness of the male and female bodies for sexual intercourse. He labels this as 'nuptial'.

John Paul II sets his exegesis against a background of Jesus' reply to the Pharisees, when they asked him whether it was lawful to divorce one's wife for any cause. Jesus answered, 'Have you not read that he who made them from the beginning made them male and female and said, "For this reason a man shall leave his father and mother and be joined to his wife and the two shall become one flesh?" So they are no longer two but one flesh. What God has joined together, let no man put asunder' (Matt. 19:3ff). The Pope pays particular attention to Jesus' reference to the 'beginning'. For him, this implies a basic constitutive state of nuptuality and, as we shall see below, of innocence.

Sexual intercourse and nakedness are completely free from shame or embarrassment in the setting of coitus within the context of marriage. The Pope, of course, acknowledges the fall and original sin, but he sees in Christ a resumption with that link of innocence.

Genesis 2:18–25 doesn't refer to procreation, rather it focuses on the significance of intercourse for the sake of the union of the couple. It is interesting that the oldest account of sexual intercourse should concentrate on the relational meaning of the act. It is the body that transacts this union through which the couple donate the whole of themselves to each other. Through the body there is an encounter of persons and in this meeting the genitals transmit the whole richness of each to the other.

It could be argued that the text as it stands does not concentrate on the relational aspect of the act, but on the need for the provision of a helper suitable for man. In this sense the woman could be defined as a helper, a subordinate to the man to meet his sexual and other needs. But the passage starts with Yahweh God's comment that it is not right for man to be alone. John Paul II comments that this reference is a response to the initial state of mankind moving from original solitude to unity. From what has been said, it is not unreasonable to assume that the creation of woman is an act of mutual communion between equals. In this communion of persons, sexual intercourse is a focus of communication. John Paul II argues extensively in favour of this interpretation: 'In sexual self-donation the couple indeed speak a "language of the body", expressing in a manner far more profound than words, the totality of the gift of each other.' However, one would need to read *The Theology of the Body* to follow his closely argued case.

Beyond Genesis, I believe that the whole Bible suggests a psycho-somatic-spiritual unity of man and woman, of which sexual intercourse can be said to be a focal point. It would require a scriptural scholar to analyse in detail the evidence in favour of this view in the Scriptures, but an outline of the case can be made from Genesis 2:18–25.

In the course of history this insight into the mutual donation of self became overshadowed by the emphasis on transmission of life and childbearing through sexual intercourse. It is only in our own day that coitus has become detached from the intimate link with childbearing so as to free it to return to its original meaning, the communication of life in its widest personal sense.

Genesis 1:26–31, the so-called priestly narrative, written some five centuries later, supplements the first account with distinctive additions.

God said, 'Let us make man in our own image, in the likeness of ourselves, and let them be masters of the fish of the sea, the birds of heaven, the cattle, all the wild animals and all the reptiles that crawl upon the earth.'

God created man in the image of himself,
in the image of God he created him,
male and female he created them.

God blessed them, saying to them, 'Be fruitful, multiply, fill the earth and conquer it. Be masters of the fish of the sea, the birds of heaven and all the living creatures that move on the earth.'

God also said, 'See I give you all the seed-bearing plants that are upon the whole earth, and all the trees with seed-bearing fruit; this shall be your food. To all the wild beasts, all birds of heaven and all living reptiles on the earth I give all the foliage of plants for food.' And so it was. God saw all he had made, and indeed it was very good. (Gen. 1:26–31)

In this second and later passage, God confirms the creation of man and woman and the author here adds that the couple reflected the image of God in them. We can inescapably conclude that sexuality is to be found in the Godhead. Critics would say that if this conclusion was inescapable, it should have been drawn a long time ago and it was not. My reply would be that if the couple reflect the image of God in them then this would also include sexuality, but that the traditional hostility to sexuality made this interpretation difficult.

In this passage, sexuality is focused on procreation, on children, and this interpretation of its meaning was held steadfastly for 3,000 years. Procreation within the context of marriage was the primary meaning given to sexuality. Yet this is not what the passage proclaims. It states that God saw all he had made and found it very good, and that includes sexuality. The interpretation that Christianity found in the course of time was that only marriage makes intercourse good. Whilst the two texts suggest that marriage is the context for sexual intercourse, as procreation needs parents to nurture children, traditional Christian interpretation has tended to dismiss the value that sexual intercourse has in itself as part of what God saw and found very good. In other words the value of sexual intercourse in its own right was not recognised and appreciated until our own time. This book is devoted to an exposition of the intrinsic value of coitus.

In the Old Testament the increase of the chosen people was of great importance and childbearing received much praise. As Rebekah leaves her family to marry Isaac, she is bidden 'Sister of ours, from you may there spring many thousands and tens of thousands' (Gen. 24:60). Both Abraham and Isaac are promised that their posterity would be as countless as the stars in the sky (Gen. 15:5; 22:17). 'The crown of the aged is their children's children' (Prov.

17:6). 'Happy is the man who has his quiver full of them' (Ps. 127:3–5). Infertility, on the other hand, was seen as a disgrace, a punishment from God. Just as Yahweh rewards sexuality by giving children, so he punishes aspects of sexual conduct. If we confine ourselves to heterosexual behaviour, then the prime condemnation was focused on incest, adultery and prostitution. Why were these patterns of behaviour condemned and on what basis?

In his fascinating book, *Dirt, Greed and Sex*,[2] L. W. Countryman suggests that the grounds for sexual condemnation in ancient Israel were based on purity and property. Based on the work of Mary Douglas, *Purity and Danger*,[3] Countryman postulates that sexual impurity is found in the difference between cleanliness and uncleanliness. One of the easiest of the purity principles to understand is the concern about menstruating women. In Israel, during her menstruation, a woman was unclean for seven days and her uncleanness was contagious, so that others became infected if they touched any furniture on which the menstruating women had lain. The uncleanness extends to a woman who has a haemorrhage. In this respect we see the extent to which Jesus overcame the purity laws about cleanliness, not only in his teaching of the apostles, but also in the fact that he allowed his garment to be touched by a woman who had an issue of blood (Mark 5:34). Summing up the idea of dirt emanating from purity principles, Countryman has this to say: 'What is consistent from one culture to another is that purity rules relate to the boundaries of the human body, especially to its orifices. This means that whatever passes these boundaries has particular importance for purity laws: foods, waste products, shed blood, menstrual blood, sexual emissions, sexual acts, birth, death.' Countryman makes it very clear that purity laws were one source for dictating sexual conduct in Israel. Thus incest, adultery and prostitution were all considered defiling.

As mentioned above, Jesus went beyond the purity laws. In an important passage in Matthew, Jesus called the people to him and said, 'Listen, and understand. What goes into the mouth does not make a man unclean; it is what comes out of the mouth that makes him unclean' (Matt. 15:10–11). The apostles, steeped in Jewish purity mentality, did not appreciate what Jesus was saying and asked him to explain. At their request, he gave his famous reply, 'Can't you see that whatever goes into the mouth passes through the stomach and is discharged into the sewer? But what comes out from the mouth comes from the heart, and it is this that makes someone unclean. For from the heart come evil intentions: murder, adultery, fornication, theft, perjury, slander. These are the things that make a person unclean. But eating with unwashed hands does not make anyone unclean' (Matt. 15:17–20). In a profound psychological shift, Jesus put the emphasis of sexual sin not on physical purity, but on feelings, motivation and the will, all emanating from the inner world of human beings. This move from physical dirt to purity of heart did not stop Christianity from casting women in general – and menstruating ones in particular – as objects of uncleanliness to be avoided. The long history of looking at women in terms of danger, and experiencing their bodies as a threat, stems from the purity laws. In its history, Christianity was to deviate far from the directness and clarity of the original description of the body and the two sexes in the passages in Genesis.

Countryman puts forward a second principle responsible for sexual conduct, namely that of property. Israel was based on the principle of patriarchy. The husband was the head of the household and his wife, children, slaves and animals were his property. Children, like wives, were foremost possessions. Once again Countryman shows that incest, adultery and prostitution contravened property principles. Thus adultery was a violation of the property of another and was punishable by stoning. Indeed, in John's gospel the scribes and Pharisees brought such a woman to Jesus (John 8:3–11). It is no exaggeration to assert that in Jesus' handling of the woman he not only reasserted the principles of compassion, forgiveness and love, but he also attacked the context of sexual sin in terms of property.

Indeed we know that Jesus set a much higher standard. 'You have heard how it was said, you shall not commit adultery. But I say this to you, if a man looks at a woman lustfully he has already committed adultery with her in his heart' (Matt. 5:27–28). In *The Theology of the Body*, John Paul II devotes a whole section to this passage of Jesus. A superficial reading of the passage might imply that it is wrong to disrupt another marriage and thus commit adultery, but the Pope comments extensively on this. He stresses that the adultery of a lustful look is in the heart. By lust is meant an experience of sexual desire devoid of a loving relationship. According to the Pope, lust is a break of the nuptial unity, of the communion between man and woman. The nuptial unity of the body stressed by Jesus in the 'beginning' is a unity of the physical, social, psychological and cognitive aspects of man and woman offered mutually in an exclusive relationship of love. The lustful look that Jesus refers to in the heart as adultery, is a solely physical sexual attraction which enjoys the other person as an object, but which has no mutuality of personal gift. Jesus assumed that a woman is not primarily a piece of property who is violated by being taken from the rightful possession of another. She is a person who deserves love, and anyone who treats her with sexual desire devoid of love has offended against her. Thus as we move from the Old to the New Testament, we see that the two pillars on which sexual transgression were based, namely purity (dirt) and possession, were modified by Jesus. In one form or another they were to remain in force until our day, although Jesus put love, intention and will in their place.

Moving to the New Testament, there is not much written specifically about sexual intercourse. There are three features related to it. The first is the virgin birth of Jesus. In my book, *One Like Us*,[4] I deal with the nurturing aspects of the parenting of Jesus rather than emphasising virginity per se. The important thing from Jesus' point of view was that he had a set of parents who made it possible for him to develop his loving side to the point where he was love and God's nature of love could coexist easily with his human nature.

The second point made in the New Testament is Jesus' introduction of the single state dedicated to God. After Jesus forbade divorce (Matt. 19:1–9), the apostles said to him, 'If that is how things are between husband and wife, it is advisable not to marry.' But he replied, 'It is not everyone who can accept what I have said, but only those to whom it is granted. There are eunuchs born so from their mother's womb. There are eunuchs made so by human agency and there are eunuchs who have made themselves so for the sake of the kingdom of heaven. Let anyone accept this who can' (Matt. 19:10–12). This concept of continence, or exercising self-control, for the sake of the kingdom of God is a new one introduced by Jesus. Those who have made it a basis for affirming the single state have often failed to notice how clear Jesus was to show that it is a gift, a rare gift, granted to the few chosen by God. Compulsion has no place in its ranks. Nevertheless, combined with the virgin birth, it brought a new vision away from sexual intercourse to continence.

The third point that needs to be made is that we have no evidence that Jesus married or had sexual intercourse. In my book I point out that, although he neither married nor, as far as we know, had sexual intercourse, there is no reason to suggest that he did not have ordinary sexual feelings. But marriage, sexual intercourse, children and family would have been too restrictive for the man who came to serve the whole world, to be open to all mankind throughout the ages.

Thus from Jesus himself we associate virginity in his parents, the pursuit of continence for the kingdom and the absence of marriage in himself. What about marriage and sexual intercourse in the New Testament? For the fullest treatment of this we must turn to Paul and in particular to his first letter to the Corinthians. It would appear that the Corinthians, as all the early Christians, were waiting for an early return of Jesus. Paul makes it clear that they should live as if they were living in the last days. But does this mean they should abandon marriage and sexual intercourse? Not at all. 'Now for the questions about which you wrote, yes it is a good thing for a man not to touch a woman; yet to avoid immorality every man should have his own wife and every woman her own husband' (1 Cor. 7:1–3).

Paul approves of the single state. He adds, 'To the unmarried and the widows I say: It is good for them to stay as they are, like me. But if they cannot exercise self-control, let them marry, since it is better to be married than to be burnt up' (1 Cor. 7:8–9). Paul is pragmatic. He appreciates that men and women have sexual drives which most of them need to express. He would prefer that they remain unmarried, but he does not make impossible demands and prefers marriage to fornication and adultery.

Regarding frequency of intercourse, he says: 'The husband must give to his wife what she has a right to expect and so the wife to her husband. The wife does not have authority over her own body, but the husband does; and in the same way, the husband does not have authority over his own body, but the wife does. You must not deprive each other, except by mutual consent for a limited time, to leave yourself free for prayer and to come together again afterwards; otherwise Satan may take advantage of any lack of self-control to put you to the test' (1 Cor. 7:3–6).

In these few lines Paul shows himself a master of sexual understanding. Spouses are to have access to one another, a model of equality. He says that they should not deprive each other, except for prayer. Paul is not counselling continence for the married. He accepts sexual desire and encourages its free expression. Later on in the same letter he repeats the same points: although time is short, everyone should remain in the state they were called to. 'If you are joined to a wife, do not seek to be released; if you are freed of a wife, do not look for a wife. However, if you do get married, that is not a sin, and it is not sinful for a virgin to enter upon marriage' (1 Cor. 7:27–28).

From this letter to the Corinthians, we get a picture of Paul in which he shows a realistic acknowledgement of sexual needs. To those who have them, marriage is a way of meeting them. He is not enthusiastic about matrimony but he appreciates human reality. He favours the single state as a way of serving the Lord. Remaining single for the sake of the Lord is his own option. Paul appears not to have received any clear instruction on virginity. 'About people remaining virgin, I have no directions from the Lord, but I give my own opinion as a person who has been granted God's mercy to be faithful' (1 Cor. 7:25).

At the end of the gospels and the epistles, we have a picture in which sexual intercourse embedded in marriage is a norm that is accepted. Jesus carried out his first miracle at the wedding feast of Cana (John 2:1–11). He would not have participated at a wedding if he did not wish to continue the state of marriage and, within it, sexual intercourse.

Sexual intercourse was understood by Paul as a natural and God-given expression to meet sexual needs. But, independent of Jesus, he initiated a tradition of the single state dedicated to God that was to span the whole of the next 2,000 years to our very day.

In Genesis we find God seeing all that he had created as very good. That included sexual intercourse, but there was no special analysis of coitus. The nearest we get to a link between sex and love is the indirect symbolism of marriage as a covenant relationship between Yahweh and Israel. The book of the prophet Hosea describes the adultery of his wife, and Yahweh's instruction to take her back and be reconciled in a spirit of tenderness and love. Here, as in the case of the Song of Songs, which we shall be examining later, marriage and sex are seen in emotional terms of love. But, apart from these two Old Testament descriptions, sexual intercourse is not seen primarily in personal terms. The two Testaments form the background for the pessimism and ambivalence with which sexuality was to be held for most of the Christian period. In the next chapter, we turn to the first five centuries of the Christian era in which sexual intercourse was immersed in a particular gloom.

Chapter 2

The Early Centuries

The Christian era was inaugurated against a backdrop of the expectation of the imminent second coming or *parousia*. The Pauline letters were full of exhortations which took their reference from the belief that time was short. With this view in mind, Paul encouraged the early Christians to stay in the state he found them in and, as far as the married were concerned, to continue to remain in marriage with sexual intercourse as one of its expressions. But as he expected the second coming, he recommended those who were not married to remain single.

With the passage of time, the expectation of the second coming faded. Men and women were not exempt from sexual urges and needs. How did their leaders attempt to shape their sexual behaviour? These men (because the leaders were all men) had to work with the 'givens' of the Christian faith: the virgin birth of Jesus; his single state; his ideas on the single state dedicated to God, and the teaching of Genesis that recommended marriage as a source of companionship and procreation. The classic study of Peter Brown in the book *The Body and Society*[1] offers, at the present time of writing, the clearest and most extensive presentation of how the first five centuries up to St Augustine developed the theme of sexuality. Those who are interested in this fascinating study are recommended to read the book itself. Here a brief summary is given of the views and influence of the main actors on the stage.

The work of Brown can be divided into the views of eminent fathers and the consequences of monastic life in the desert. This took place in a Roman context, which saw marriage as the beginning, root and fountainhead of human nature. It is from marriage that fathers, mothers, children and families spring. Children were a necessity in an age when life expectancy was on average less than 25 years, and when only 4 out of every 100 men and fewer women lived beyond the age of 50. Sexual intercourse and reproduction were regarded as essential for the maintenance of the population. Although sexual intercourse in the service of reproduction was considered the norm, there were two classic attitudes operating as well. The first was a powerful belief that the body was made up of vital spirit and its loss devitalised it. Hence all loss of vital spirit, including emission of seed, weakened the body. The second was the Stoic philosophy that what was best for human beings was a strict control of the emotions that led to *apatheia*. The mature person had all his or her emotions under strict control and was indifferent to them. Soranus is quoted as saying, 'Men who remain chaste are stronger and better than others and pass their lives in better health.'[2] This view is not supported by modern research. For the Stoics, sexual intercourse was supposed to occur only for reproduction, an idea that heavily influenced early Christianity. There was no concept of coitus for pleasure and the positions adopted for intercourse were to be selected on the basis of the best deposition of the seed for fecundity. The marital bed was no place for pleasure but for orderly activity designed for procreation.

The Greek and Latin fathers, particularly the latter, took their cue from their Christian background of virginity, the apotheosis of the single state and the classical views outlined above, so that, writing at the end of the second century, Clement of Alexandria could say, 'The human ideal of continence, I mean that which is set forth by the Greek philosophers, teaches one to resist passion, so as not to be made subservient to it, and to train the instincts to pursue rational goals.' But for Christians he went on to say, 'Our ideal is not to experience desire at all' (quoted in Brown). The last sentence gives a flavour of what the fathers thought about human sexuality. One of the marks of identification with the Holy Spirit was sexual abstinence.

We begin with the figure of Tertullian in the late second century. His commands give us a glimpse of the admixture on sexual writings that were circulating in a major Latin Church, Carthage. Tertullian was a Stoic and he concentrated on the body. His deceptively simple formula was 'Look to the body', and for him continence brought down the gift of the Holy Spirit. If sanctity was not to be obtained through martyrdom, then continence was the next best thing. Tertullian was the first to make this important statement, which had a long influence in the Latin world, that abstinence from sex was the most effective way to achieve clarity of the soul. The teaching of Tertullian and other fathers we shall consider below enunciated the theology, but the practice was seen in members of the Christian communities throughout the Mediterranean in the second and third centuries, who expressed with vehemence their belief in continence by their renunciation of married life. In the less orthodox circles, the Gnostic and Manichean theologies propagated similar views of abandoning marriage.

Also towards the end of the second century Clement of Alexandria, one of the most prolific writers of the pre-Constantine Church, arrived on the scene. He stressed the importance of every moment of daily life, especially the life of the household. Clement acknowledged human sexual urges, but put forward the view that they were to be strictly disciplined. He was a wholehearted supporter of the Stoic view of *apatheia*, the idea of a life free from passions. And so he advocated a serenity in sexual behaviour as in all other aspects of life – order in everything as well as in sexual activity. His concept of disciplined order was to avoid frequent intercourse, not to use a variety of positions to maximise pleasure and to avoid intercourse when one's wife was pregnant. No such liberties were allowed for Christians. Sexual intercourse should take place for procreation and not for aesthetic pleasure.

For Origen in the early third century sexuality was a mere passing phase. Human beings could do without it. In order to give expression to his view of sexuality as a transient entity of no importance to the spirit, he had himself castrated. As a natural consequence of these ideas he advocated continence from an early stage of life. Virginity stood for the original state and reflected the purity of the soul. Ultimately, he believed that all physical relations would vanish. Sexual intercourse, Origen believed, as many subsequently have, coarsened the spirit. Virgin bodies were temples of God. As with Tertullian, this theology had practical applications and perpetual continence was upheld by groups of Christians throughout the

Mediterranean. Origen died in AD 253 and by then the combined efforts of Tertullian, Clement of Alexandria and himself had set the tone for the preference for virginity and continence.

In AD 306 the Synod of Elvira declared that 'Bishops, priests, deacons and all members of the clergy connected with the Liturgy must abstain from their wives and must not beget sons.'[3] By the beginning of the fourth century, two things had been established. The clergy were encouraged not to marry or, if married, not to have sexual intercourse, and a close link was made between liturgy and the avoidance of sexuality.

Brown comments that by the end of the second century it might have been possible for Christianity to develop based on the family and protected, albeit with demanding limitations, by a view of sexuality as outlined by Clement of Alexandria. It would have been linked with rigorous discipline and fear of women, but would have not progressed in favour of the total renunciation of sexual activity. Instead total sexual renunciation had become widely acclaimed as a feature of the Christian life. Brown, however, adds that it was a renunciation limited to the few, even though they saw themselves as the elite.

Still in the fourth century we find another theological giant, Gregory of Nyssa. Sexuality for Gregory was an afterthought of the creator. It had been added to the original serene indifferentiation of nature, along with death, after Adam's fall. Sexual differentiation was a necessary adjustment after the Fall. Gregory was preoccupied with the clock of life, which measured the passage of tainted time and he situated this clock in marriage. He saw human time made up of attempts to block out the sight of the grave. Marriage and sexual intercourse and the raising of children were such a pastime. So the removal of sexuality was the denial of time, placed there by the fear of death – remove marriage and you remove the one institution that had been brought about by death. Adam and Eve recognised their fear of extinction and joined together in marriage to have children. And so for Gregory the tick of time lay silent in the heart of the continent person.

Gregory's view was reinforced in the same century by that of John Chrysostom, the most gifted preacher of his age. For Chrysostom marriage was a superfluity rendered necessary only by the fall of

Adam. In his book on virginity he declared that the earth was already overpopulated and needed no further reproductive effort.

Moving from East to West, we meet in the fourth century Ambrose, Bishop of Milan, who was particularly sensitive to the weaknesses of the flesh. For him, the body was a peril that might engulf the soul. Every human being bore an ugly scar and that scar was sexuality. For Ambrose, Christ was the perfect model, unscarred by a sexual origin and the presence of sexual impulses. Ambrose, among others, was a champion of the continence of bishops and clergy, providing a separate, hierarchical class of the ascent of life. On his scale, virgins came first, widows second and the married third. The integrity of the virgin state was the highest pinnacle of Christian virtue.

Finally, we have in Jerome in the late fourth century an ardent apostle for virginity. He was the heir of Origen and he communicated vividly the awareness of the sexual dangers of the body. For Jerome the human body was a darkened forest filled with the roaring of wild beasts that could only be controlled by rigid diet and the strict avoidance of sexual attraction. For him, even first marriages were regrettable but second ones were only one step away from the brothel.

During the centuries covered by the lives of these fathers, others left the city and settled in the desert, forming monastic communities. These were the desert fathers of whom the best known was Anthony. For the monks of Egypt, sexual temptation was a drive towards women and matrimony, and hence a return to settled land and away from the desert. For the desert ascetic, whilst sexuality was a temptation, the urge for food was an even greater challenge. It was widely believed by the desert fathers that the first sin of Adam and Eve was not sexual, but ravenous greed. So fasting was at the forefront of their life. Food pushed sexuality aside. Thus self-mortification in terms of food and sex was the first line of attack on the senses. When the body was quelled, it was the heart and the will that had to be subdued. From the heart and the will emerged pride and ambition, and the combination of these could destroy monastic communities. From the heart and the will emanated sexual fantasies and it was finally the abatement of fantasy that was the proof of the conquering of sexuality. The overcoming of sexuality was associated with the cessation of nocturnal emissions. Control over the body was the monk's preoccupation. The desert ascetic did not flourish with just control over his mind. His body also had to be tutored and in bringing the body under control the soul was influenced. The material life of the monk was considered capable of altering consciousness. Between them the fathers and the desert monks influenced the climate of sexuality of the first five centuries and left an enduring legacy in the West.

The last father to be considered is Augustine, the giant of them all.[4] He wrote the definitive book on marriage, whose ends of children, faithfulness and permanency had a profound impact on Christianity and was quoted as recently as Pius XI's encyclical *Casti Connubii* in 1930.[5]

Augustine knew that sexual intercourse was deeply associated with pleasure. He had experienced this pleasure over a period of 13 years with a woman. During these years, he associated with the Manicheans and tried to control his sexual urges, but all to no avail. His sexual drive was strong and, in the immortal words that have often been quoted, he wrote in his confessions, 'Lord, give me chastity and continence, but not now.'[6] His mother, Monica, prayed relentlessly for his conversion and he parted from the woman in order to get married. Even during the period of waiting for the marriage, he could not control his sexual urges and took a concubine. Finally, he converted to Christianity, gave up the idea of marriage and close association with women, and went on to serve his God with distinction.

Augustine, holding a contemporary minority view, believed that there would have been sexual relations between Adam and Eve before the Fall. His original and devastating view was formulated round his concept of original sin. Whilst agreeing that this would involve the loss of sanctifying grace, he was convinced that an even greater result would be the loss of an effective ordering of man's passions leading to concupiscence or sexual desire. He associated concupiscence with intercourse and thought that coitus transmitted original sin. Thus sexual intercourse was always accompanied by sin. But, if sex was performed for procreation, this sinfulness was reduced; for any other reason it remained at least venially or pardonably sinful.

We have to see in this theology not only spiritual speculation but psychological overreaction to coitus that shows itself in the following passage: 'As to copulation in marriage which, according to the law of matrimony must be used for procreation's sake; does it not seek a corner for its performance, though it be honest and lawful? Does not the bridegroom turn all the servants, and even the bridesmaids and all others, out of his chamber, before he begins to embrace his bride? As the great author of Roman eloquence has said, whereas all honest deeds desire the light, that is love to be known, this only desires so to be known that it blushes to be seen ... For this act desires indeed to be seen by the mind, yet it seeks to escape from the sight of the eye. Now what can be the reason for this, unless it be that this lawful act of nature is accompanied with a penalty of shame from our first parents?'[7] It is significant that Christianity has not followed Augustine in either of these propositions: that sexual intercourse in marriage is in any way sinful or that it transmits original sin. The vehemence with which he expressed these views does suggest, however, that Augustine was working out in his theology his own psychological problems. With Augustine, we reach the peak of pessimism and negativity about sexual intercourse.

The first five centuries produced a series of theological treatises that devalued coitus, saw virginity and continence as higher states, influenced the avoidance of sexual intercourse by the clergy and the downgrading of coitus.

The Stoic view of emotional tranquillity coupled with Jesus' single state, the virginity of his mother, the apparent immanent second coming and the idiosyncratic views of individual theologians, combined to cast sexuality and coitus in a negative light, from which Christianity is perhaps only emerging in our own day and time.

The devaluation of one of God's most precious gifts started in these early centuries and produced a massive distortion of the goodness of sex. We shall see that in the subsequent centuries, although modifications took place, the basic negativity never gave up its relentless grip.

The patristic period thus concluded in a spirit of asceticism and sexual pessimism in which the developing attitudes to sexuality have lost, temporarily in the writings of the fathers and others, the links with the positive approach of the Old Testament. Sexual intercourse came under the influence of Hellenistic dualism,

Stoicism, which had infiltrated Christian thought, the growing importance of the single state dedicated to God and the personal experience of such men as Tertullian, Jerome and Augustine. Thus the Christian era began under a cloud of sexual pessimism that cast a long shadow to this very day.

Chapter 3

The Medieval Period

The medieval period saw a mixture of a reiteration of the rigorism of the early Church with the return to Augustinian theology and a softening of attitudes. Augustine set a very exacting standard for the interpretation of the meaning of sexual intercourse, which was bound to influence later theologians. One of these was Gregory I, Pope from 590 to 604, a man of outstanding talent, whose 850 surviving letters and other writings had a considerable influence in the Middle Ages. He followed the Augustinian approach in general but changed the details. He stated that whilst the sexual act in itself was not sinful – nor its involvement with concupiscence – the pleasure attached to it was. So that, even when spouses desired children, they could not avoid the inevitable pleasure attached to the act, which was sinful.[1] With this view, which once again would find no permanent place in the teaching of the Church, the theology of the sexual act reached its lowest ebb. This Gregorian view – that all sexual pleasure was an evil – reached its maximum strength at the end of the twelfth century. In this teaching, a value for sexual intercourse such as love was unthinkable.

Against this solid opposition to the link between coitus and love, there emerged in the second quarter of the twelfth century a new ideology, which was opposed to the link between sexual intercourse and procreation. It was the code of courtly love, sung by many of the troubadours. The troubadours praised the love of man for woman. They separated love from marriage, celebrating sexual pleasure and rejecting the generative purpose. By 1139, the level of danger of such a view drew the attention of the Ecumenical Council, the Second Lateran Council, who reiterated the orthodox position.

The development of the procreative purpose of marriage and sex in the twelfth century was a reaction to the Cathars and courtly love. The emerging doctrine vigorously excluded pleasure as a purpose of sexual intercourse. There were two basic reasons for the return of such strictness. The first was a response to the Cathars and the second a return to Augustinian sexual ethics. In this doctrine coitus was found to be reprehensible and evil, unless excused by the Augustinian goods of marriage. According to this more rigid view, some small sin was inevitable in coitus.

Thomas Aquinas (1225–74) contributed a mixture of traditional and more optimistic views on sexual intercourse. The basic assumptions held by Aquinas were that natural coitus was instituted by God and that the natural order should not be altered by man. For him, the natural order of sexual intercourse demanded no other position for coitus than the woman beneath the man. He used the word 'bestiality' to characterise modes of sexual intercourse that depart from this position.

The Thomistic analysis takes the biological function of procreation of the sexual act as given by God and unalterable by man. 'The end, however, which nature intends in copulation is offspring to be procreated and educated and that this good might be sought it has put delight in copulation, as Augustine says, in marriage and concupiscence. Whoever, therefore uses copulation for the delight which is in it, not referring the intention to the end intended by nature acts against nature.'[2] The position taken in intercourse, its purpose and its delight were strictly for procreation. This attitude, which Aquinas formulated, reinforcing Augustine's view, was to remain supreme in official church teaching until our own day. Thus for Aquinas, a norm is postulated consisting in heterosexual, marital coitus, the man above the woman, with insemination resulting. This norm is ordained, its naturalness is established by God. Deliberate departure from the norm is unnatural, a direct offence against God. Aquinas distinguished between the delight experienced as an inducement for procreation, and the rightfulness and intensity of that delight. He argued that before the Fall there would have been more delight in coitus because of the greater purity of nature and the greater sensibility of the body. After the Fall, concupiscence detracts coitus from the command of reason. Aquinas accepted the normality of sexual pleasure. For him there was no assent to Gregorian rigorism. Dealing with the question that excess of passion corrupts virtue, he says, 'The excessive passion which corrupts virtue is one that not only hinders or prevents the exercise of reason, but also destroys the rational order, but this is not the effect of the intensity of the delight in the marriage act, for although man is not then under control, yet he has been controlled and directed beforehand by reason.'[3]

Writing 50 years ago, Father Messenger in his book *The Mystery of Sex and Marriage* went further and stated: 'Joining together all the strands of St Thomas' teaching, we can assert without hesitation that there is a very important place to be allotted to passion and pleasure in the sex act. Both passion and pleasure are natural concomitants of the sex act, and, so far from diminishing its novel goodness if the sex act is willed beforehand according to right reason, the effect of pleasure and passion is simply to heighten and increase the moral goodness of the act, not in any way to diminish it. St Thomas does not seem to say this any where expressly, but it nevertheless follows plainly and definitely from his principles, and accordingly, we ourselves have no hesitation in drawing the inference and in making the statement.'[4]

Whilst Aquinas, clarified by Messenger, portrayed a benevolent moral stance of coitus if carried out for procreation, there remained in him an ambivalence about the act. He writes: 'We are joined to God, both by the habit of grace and by the act of contemplation and love. That which prevents the first kind of union is always sinful, but that which prevents the second kind is not always sinful, for there are certain lawful occupations concerning inferior matters which distract the soul and make it unworthy of being joined actually to God and this is especially the case with the sex act, in which the mind is held because of intense pleasure. For this reason those to whom it belongs to contemplate divine things, or to perform sacred functions, are instructed to abstain from their wives at that time.'[5] Aquinas in his strictly analytical and rational approach considered coitus to be morally good. In his social and subjective view he considered intercourse an inferior matter.

The suspicion with which the medieval theologians approached sexual intercourse is shown further in the fact that they advocated abstinence in the seasons of fasting and on certain festivals, also on Thursday in memory of Christ's arrest, on Friday in memory of his death, on Saturday in honour of Our Lady, on Sunday in honour of the resurrection and on Monday in commemoration of the departed! Although such spiritual counsels are part of the documented history, there is very little evidence to assess how closely such advice was followed by the people.

Indeed, others suggested less demanding requirements. We find William of Auvergne, Archbishop of Paris in the early thirteenth century, observing: 'Intercourse, although it is carnal, can involve a spiritual pleasure. Every act of virtue involves pleasure, or at least is able to . . . So if the marriage act results from a concern to grant the other what is due, or from a charitable anxiety to keep oneself or one's wife from the stain of sin . . . No one should doubt that from that act there can sometimes arise a spiritual delight in the heart of the one who performs it.'[6]

This spiritual interpretation of the sexual act had another advocate in the Dutch mystic Dionysius the Carthusian (Denys van Leeuwen, 1402–71), who wrote in the *Praiseworthy Life of the Married* that marriage is a sacrament and it is good. The marital act is good and is the work of charity or spiritual love when it is performed for the paying of the marital debt, for procreation or to prevent fornication by one's spouse. Although, he added, the married can mutually love each other because of the mutual pleasure they have in the marital act, he also cautioned that the too fervent lover is an adulterer. So the ambivalence of Aquinas continued. Nevertheless, Denys attempted to bring together the spiritual and carnal love in marriage, but this had little impact.

Noonan comments 'that a new theory began its life with a man who was thoroughly and typically the product of Parisian intellectualism when the University of Paris was still the centre of European theological thought. This man was Martin Le Maistre (1432–81). His book *Moral Questions*, published posthumously in 1490, is, I believe, the most independent critique of the Christian sexual ethics undertaken by an orthodox critic.' Le Maistre sweeps away the Augustinian purposes of sexual intercourse and asserts that coitus is legitimate for repaying the marital debt and avoidance of fornication. He also introduces a new concept of seeking bodily health and an even newer one 'for calming the mind'. He denied the existing views that coitus for avoiding fornication is venial sin and sex for the sake of lust or obtaining pleasure is mortal sin. He then advanced the totally new view that sexual pleasure can be taken first for its own sake, and secondly to avoid tedium and the ache of melancholy caused by the lack of pleasure. Such views were totally radical for the period and are only consonant with contemporary thought.

Another person who had similar radical views was John Major (1470–1550), who maintained that it was no sin to have sexual intercourse to avoid fornication, for one's own or one's spouse's health, and also for the sheer pleasure of it. Le Maistre and Major challenged Augustinian views and had no patristic or other medieval support. They claimed their views emanated from reason alone, but they met with general hostility for at least a century.

In 1563 the Council of Trent became the first ecumenical council to say that husbands were to love their wives as Christ loved the Church, echoing Paul, but no connection was made between love and sexual intercourse. A little later, Sanchez (1550–1610) was to declare that couples who had sexual intercourse simply as husband and wife were not sinning. This view took further the position that there was no need to have the intention of procreation or the avoidance of fornication to have intercourse. Sanchez defended sexual contacts of spouses apart from coitus, and in doing so proclaimed love as a value. But this view was opposed and Innocent XI attacked the whole idea of sexual intercourse for pleasure alone.

Moving beyond the strict historical boundaries of the Middle Ages, Francis of Sales, at the beginning of the seventeenth century, promoted further the goodness and the holiness of sexual intercourse. In his *Introduction to The Devout Life* he says, 'Marital intercourse is certainly holy, lawful and praiseworthy in itself and profitable to society.'[7] Further, in a passage remarkable for its frankness and understanding, he writes, 'Love wedded to fidelity gives birth to a confident intimacy, so that we find saintly husbands and wives making abundant use of mutual caresses as chaste as they are loving, as tender as they are sincere, as in the case of Isaac and Rebecca, the most pure couple in ages past.' Despite this positive attitude, Francis of Sales chose an elephant as an ideal to illustrate pleasure in the sexual act. The elephant is faithful and loving to the female, but it is supposed to mate only every third year for no more than five days, secretly so as not to be seen until the sixth day. Then it goes to the river to wash itself, unwilling to return to the herd until it is purified. This, he suggested, is a good and modest habit and an example to husbands and wives!

This description of sexuality is a reflection of the ambivalence of the Middle Ages towards sexual intercourse. Undoubtedly there were advances in thought, but no close link between coitus and love was made. Although Augustine's views receded, they remained a background force. His subjective and emotive views on sexuality gave way to the rational and natural law position of Aquinas. But by this time, theology was firmly in the hands of male theologians who were celibate, in a society that was concerned with survival and not love, despite the presence of the troubadours. And so, although there was progress in the understanding of sexuality, a core view remained that linked sexual intercourse primarily with procreation and not with love.

Chapter 4

The Reformation

The Reformation saw many changes, not least in beliefs about marriage and sexuality, with Luther radically attacking the sacramental nature of marriage. 'It is nowhere written that he who takes a wife receives the grace of God.'[1] Thus the painstaking work of the theologians of the Middle Ages was nullified at a stroke.

Calvin similarly declared that although marriage was a divine ordinance, there was no evidence for a special grace-bearing character attached to marriage. These denials brought forth an unequivocal denunciation by the Council of Trent, which declared anathema anyone denying the grace-giving or sacramental nature of marriage.

Luther saw the ends of marriage very much as Augustine and Aquinas did, and much like the Catholic tradition he was repudiating. Luther however took a pessimistic view of marriage. Although he was later to marry, he saw marriage as a difficult and unpleasant way of life. He believed that, 'according to the spirit', the Christian had no need of marriage.[2] It was the Christian flesh that was corrupted and filled with evil desires that needed it. It was this disease of the flesh that required the result. The results of original sin were for him 'shame at nakedness and all things sexual, the burning of lust, the subjection of woman to man, the pangs of childbirth and the heartache of parenthood'. And so marriage was for him a medicine, 'a hospital for the sick'.[3] As far as Luther was concerned, his views on marriage and sexuality were steeped in Augustinian and patristic pessimism. The sexual act was accompanied by a sense of shame because of the loss of trust in God. It was always unclean, but nevertheless a necessity.[4] Luther had no illusions about the conception of sexual drive. Taking entirely the man's view, he saw coitus in marriage as the only remedy to the debauchery of mankind.

Calvin, on the other hand, stressed the relational aspects of marriage and saw woman as a companion for her husband and not merely as a relief for his concupiscence. He considered marriage's primary purpose as social rather than generative, and sexual intercourse as a holy and undefiled act.[5] Even this view could not escape the current belief that sexual pleasure was associated with some evil, through man's fall, even if it was not treated as sinful by God within marriage because of its positive characteristics in giving forth new life.

Among the later reformers Jeremy Taylor (1613–67) wrote *Rule and Exercises of Holy Living* and *Ductor Dubitantium* which are among the very few works that examine in detail the more intimate aspects of married life. In discussing the pleasure of sexual intercourse, Taylor says that the spouses, in seeking this pleasure, must follow the ends which hallow it, and among these are the desire for children, the avoidance of fornication, to lighten and ease the cares and sadness of household affairs and to endear each other. D. S. Bailey, an Anglican theologian writing some 40 years ago, considers that the mutual endearment of sexual intercourse offered by Taylor is probably the first overt theological recognition of the relational aspects of coitus, a theme which, as we shall see, was only developed in the last 40 years.[6]

Fuelled by the combination of weakness of the human flesh and, in Luther's eyes, the widespread failure of the clergy of his time to remain chaste, Luther proposed that clergy should marry. From the local Synod of Elvira in 306, the single state of the clergy had gathered momentum and, at the Second Lateran Council in 1139, clerical marriages were declared invalid. Historians record how difficult it had been to enforce this rule. Luther felt, in the light of what he believed about sexual desire and what he saw in practice around him, that this was an impossible rule to keep except by the very few. Between the Synod of Elvira and the Second Lateran Council, the church struggled with an unpopular restriction. Before the reforming Gregorian popes began to centralise power in Rome, most priests were married. The modern phenomenon of the celibate

Roman Catholic priest was facilitated by the seminaries set up after the Reformation. In recent times the much publicised sexual scandals of some Roman Catholic clergy remind us what a perennial problem the celibacy of priests is.

For Luther, priests were no exception to the frailties of the flesh and were as much subject to sexual desires as all other men. He condemned those who, in promoting celibacy, argued that the endurance of intense sexual frustration pleased God because of the bitterness and hardship of the suffering involved. For him, there was a minute number of true celibates. We have seen that sexual pleasure, companionship and mutual support were not acceptable reasons for any marriage, let alone a clerical one. Though he recognised procreation as a vital reason, it is not a sufficient explanation. Luther was pragmatic. Fallen and, for him, diseased man needs the sexual outlet of marriage and by 1525 Luther himself had married.

The ideas of the Reformation crossed the English Channel and clerical marriage was legalised in 1549 in England. There followed the religious turbulence of the reigns of Mary and Elizabeth. Elizabeth was not a great advocate of priestly marriage and she had to be persuaded in favour of it. The story of the struggle for married clergy in England is portrayed fully in Porter's book. Porter quotes the preamble to the 1549 legislation:

> Although it were not only better for the estimation of priests and other ministers of the church of God to live chaste, sole and separate from the company of women and the bond of marriage, but also thereby they might be better intent to the administration of the gospel, and be less intricated and troubled with the charge of a household, being free and unburdened by the care and cost of funding wife and child, and that it were most to be wished that they would willingly and of their selves endeavour themselves to a perpetual chastity abstinence from the use of women. Yet for as much as the contrary hath rather been seen, and such uncleanliness of living and other great inconveniences, not meet to be rehearsed, have followed of compelled chastity and in such laws as have prohibited those (such persons) the godly use of marriage, it were better and rather to be suffered in the commonwealth, that those which

could not contain should, after the counsels of scripture live in holy marriage, than feigned abuse with worse enormity outward chastity for single life . . .

In this passage, the denigration of women – 'use of women' meaning sexual intercourse – the absence of any affirmation of the goodness of marriage and of human sexuality are evident. Marriage of the clergy is advocated, in modern terms, for the urges of libido. The principal reason is the scandal of the lives of the clergy. So by the end of the sixteenth century, marriage for the clergy was generally achieved in England. Porter says that nevertheless Anglicanism, unlike other Protestant religions, would always retain a respect for clerical celibacy.

Did the marriage of the clergy bring about a more creative, positive understanding of sexual intercourse? Definitely not. When I started writing on marriage and sexuality in the early sixties, I was surprised by the lack of any insight into the nature of sexuality and its link with love that I found in the writings of the reformed tradition. In my clinical practice I was aware of the problematic nature that sexuality was for many Protestants. I am grateful to Porter for some understanding of the reasons for this. She sums up the marriage of the clergy at the Reformation by writing, 'To permit the clergy to marry, they (the reformers) had to establish a level of acceptance of sexual activity; they did not decide that clergy could marry because they had decided that sex was good. Far from it.'

For the reformers marriage was a cure, a preventative for the intense sexual burning 'that would otherwise drive a man to sin'. They understood the sex drive almost to a man to be diseased. To Philip Melanchthon, marriage was necessary for 'the bridling of passions'. For John Vernon, marriage is the 'lawful water to quench the fire of concupiscence'. For Matthew Parker, marriage is a 'port' for those molested with 'storms of temptation'.

The reformers, going back to Augustine, believed that the sex instinct as inserted in human nature by God had only one good purpose: procreation. Any other purpose of sex, even within marriage, was diseased due to the Fall. After the Fall, sexual intercourse, which before was faultless, simply 'ran riot'. For them sex for pleasure remained as sinful as ever and the counsel of moderation remained a yardstick. Heinrick Bullinger expressed it thus: 'Like as shamefastness, comeliness and temperance is good in everything, so it is good here also and exceeding necessary. Wedlock is honorable and holy, therefore must not we as shameless persons cast away good manners, and become like unreasonable beasts. God hath given and ordained marriage to be a remedy and medicine unto our feeble and weak flesh to suage the disquietness therefore and to the intent that we should be clean and undefiled in spirit and in body. And if we rage therewith, and be shameless in words and deeds, then our mistemperance and excess may make it evil which is good and defile it that is clean.'

Here we see the comparison of the sexual drive with animal instinct, the dangers of excess and all the ambivalence that has been noted in the previous chapters. Peter Martyr, a Reformation theologian, suggested that sex seen as a remedy for sin was an additional good of marriage. Augustine would not have thought in these terms and so in this sense the reformers advanced the theology of sex marginally.

In the light of these overall negative views, the reformers preserved the position that celibacy was superior to marriage. They were clear, however, to differentiate between the enforced celibacy of the Roman Catholic Church and the distinct state of the few who had the grace or, as we would now see it, the maturity of personality to express with full integrity the single state dedicated to God.

We can sum up the position of the Reformation on sexual intercourse by saying that it took a wholly pragmatic step forward. It established the legitimacy of clerical marriage. The main understanding for this was that man had to control his fallen sexual drive. Sexual intercourse within marriage was therefore legitimate, even though regrettable, but marital intercourse was neither unclean nor defiling. It was a necessity. Certainly no spiritual grace was seen in it. In this sense the reformers remained by and large true to Augustine.

Nowhere do we find in the reformers any understanding of sex that linked it primarily to love, interpersonal relationships, the goodness of sexual pleasure and reflecting what Genesis states, namely that everything God created was very good. There was no celebration of sexual love. Within this approach the superiority of sexual abstinence was left firmly intact.

Whilst the reformers left the inner world of sexual intercourse by and large untouched, they introduced, according to Porter, a paradigm shift. Thus some of the voices of Anglicanism, reinforced later by the Puritans and the Quakers, saw in the man–woman relationship in marriage a presence of love and loving companionship which transcended the traditional association with sin and the rectification by procreation. These Protestant beginnings were to flourish in the twentieth century. Nevertheless it took another 300 years for the inner world of sexuality to begin to be analysed and the next and final chapter in this historical section is dedicated to it.

Chapter 5

The Twentieth Century

Although the major movements in understanding human sexuality took place in the twentieth century, the antecedents started in the nineteenth. Biologically, the principal finding of the nineteenth century was the discovery of the Graafian follicle in the female that under hormonal stimulation induces ovulation, essential for fertilisation. This discovery brought to an end the very influential view that it was the male sperm alone that produced a whole life, the woman only nurturing it. The understanding of the female's contribution to new life brought about by this discovery was a positive start in the current context of the battle for egalitarian relationships between the sexes.

At the psychological level, the giant who overlapped the nineteenth and twentieth centuries was Sigmund Freud (1856–1939). He was the single most important contributor to the sexual revolution of the twentieth century. In his book *The Sex Researchers*, Brecher[1] points out, however, that there were others besides Freud who challenged Victorian suppression of sexuality. Havelock Ellis's (1859–1939) *Studies in the Psychology of Sex*, which first appeared in German in 1896 and in English the following year, was standard reading for those interested in the subject for several decades. Kraft-Ebing (1840–1902) wrote *Psychopathis Sexualis* in 1886 which to this very day remains the essential text for abnormal sexuality. The Dutch gynaecologist, Theodoor Hendrik van de Velde (1873–1937), informed thousands, if not millions, of couples about sexuality in marriage in his book *Ideal Marriage*.

In modern times, Alfred Charles Kinsey (1895–1956), an American, astonished the United States and the rest of the world with his statistical studies on male and female sexuality. There is no doubt that these two studies, which are still quoted, brought into the open the incidence of sexual practices, including homosexuality, which were unknown until his publications. There followed the work of Masters and Johnson in the sixties that clarified the inner world of the orgasm, in a book entitled *Human Sexual Response* in 1966. Since the sixties, there have been several other studies but the above were the seminal ones.

There is no doubt that the most influential person was Freud, who propagated the view that sexuality was an intrinsic part of the human personality and an inescapable expression of what it is to be human. He brought to an end 2,000 years of Christian suspicion of sexuality. Today we take for granted that sexuality permeates all aspects of human relationship and is not an inferior concept, delineated as lust, or merely an essential requirement of the reproduction of the species.

With the work of Masters and Johnson in the sixties, we come to our modern era, characterised by the introduction and rapid spread of the contraceptive pill which has created a permanent transformation in sexual behaviour. Concurrently with the advent of the contraceptive pill, the period of the sixties and seventies has been portrayed as the sexual revolution. It ushered in an era, still with us, which liberated sex from many taboos. Dress is much more sexually revealing. Communication is infinitely more frank and open. The world of the cinema and television is much more daring with sexual topics. Gains were made in sexual justice and equality, as for example for sexual minorities, and women's emancipation came of age. Hardly a week passes without newspapers having an article on sex. We now live in a world saturated with the subject.

At the same time as this revolution has taken place, sex has been trivialised. The philosophy of *Playboy* magazine, multiplied in numerous pornographic images, emphasises the body as a pleasure machine. Education at school has focused on the biology of sex without an associated emotional or loving component. The prevailing view is that transient sex is valid and there is an emphasis on the use of contraceptives simply to avoid procreation and disease. Sexual intercourse is understood entirely in terms of procuring an orgasm and its relational character, although acknowledged, is placed as a secondary phenomenon. In common language, 'to have a shag' is the ideal often floated across the media. Men and women, particularly the latter, are treated as sexual objects. This objectification of bodies, especially female ones, divested from relationship is portrayed widely in prostitution and pornography, both of which have become big business. Thus there is no doubt that this last century has seen a big movement in sexual awareness, accelerated in the last forty years. How have the Christian Churches responded to this historical avalanche?

For those who want to examine the Church's response in detail, reference should be made to Father Kevin T. Kelly, an eminent Roman Catholic theologian, whose book *New Directions in Sexual Ethics*[2] illustrates the history of the last 40 years very well and I am grateful to him for the information I include below. A summary of the Roman Catholic position is made by Gareth Moore, in Chapter 16 of the book *Christian Ethics*.[3] An up-to-date commentary on what the Churches say about sex is to be found in the work of Stuart and Thatcher in the book *People of Passion*.[4]

The events of the last 40 years in the area of sexuality are so extensive that only those focused on coitus are considered and only in a summary form. Contraception remains a crucial issue for Christians in that the primary purpose of sexual intercourse was seen to be procreation, and the unity between coitus and new life was seen as inviolate. As we shall see in Chapter 20, this is the position of the Roman Catholic Church to this very day. The Church of England held Lambeth Conferences in 1867 and 1897, but there was no mention of contraception on these occasions. In 1908 it was considered and an unconditional condemnation given. In 1920 there was still opposition, but in 1930 there was a vote in favour by a majority of 193 to 67. Here is the critical resolution: 'Where there is clearly felt moral obligation to limit or avoid parenthood, the method must be decided on Christian principles. The primary and obvious method is complete abstinence from intercourse (as far as may be possible) in a life of discipline and self-control lived in the power of the Holy Spirit. Nevertheless, in those cases where there is such a clearly felt moral obligation to limit or avoid parenthood, and where there is a morally sound reason for avoiding complete abstinence, the Conference agrees that other methods may be used, provided this is done in the light of the same Christian principles. The Conference reports its strongest condemnation of the use of any methods of contraception control for motives of selfishness, luxury or mere convenience.'[5]

This advance in practice, just as with the changes at the Reformation that allowed priests to marry, was not associated with any detailed examination of the inner world of sexual intercourse. The bishops at the Conference, however, declared that coitus had a value of its own in marriage, strengthening and enhancing married love, but no radical changes in sexual theology or philosophy were made at this stage. In response to this initiative Pius XI for the Catholic Church replied with the encyclical *Casti Connubii* in 1930, in which he condemned any use of contraception. He wrote: 'The conjugal act is of its very nature designed for the procreation of offspring, and therefore those, who in performing it, deliberately deprive it of its natural power and efficacy, act against nature and do something which is shameful and intrinsically immoral.' The encyclical was not just condemnatory; Pius XI went on to extend the understanding of marriage in terms of the mutual perfection of the spouses.

Encouraged by this, the Catholic theologian Doms wrote: 'We may now go on to say that there is a meaning imminent not only in the biological act (coitus) but also in marriage itself. But the meaning is not, as has often been thought, merely "love". It is rather that fulfilment of love in the community of life of two persons who make one person. This community involves the whole human being in spirit, sense and body . . . This inner meaning of marriage includes the performance of the sexual act, although it has no conscious interest in procreation. . . .'[6] Doms' book was very persuasive and his thoughts on marriage as a community of the life of two persons, reinforced by intercourse, were well in advance of his time and subsequently influenced the formulations of the Second Vatican Council. Thus we see in the thirties the progress of the relationship of husband and wife as love in action in which sexual intercourse contributes in a basic way. The thirties, forties and fifties were important in the Catholic Church for the debate on the understanding of the ends of marriage and on the use of the infertile period for regulating births. I have discussed this historic period in my first book on marriage.[7]

We can now move to the sixties and two important statements. The first is the Lambeth Conference of 1958, at which one committee produced *The Family in Contemporary Society*,[8] a document full of wisdom. In it sexual intercourse is seen as the full giving and receiving of a whole person without any false sense of fears of what is evil. Husband and wife become two in one flesh in a reaffirmed lifelong union of indissolubility.

Shortly afterwards, in the Second Vatican Council, the Roman Catholic Church dropped the terms primary and secondary ends for marriage and embraced an understanding of marriage as a community of love. This love the Lord has judged worthy of special gifts: healing, perfecting and exalting gifts of grace and of charity (Pastoral Constitution Part 2, chapter 1). Moving from marriage to sexual intercourse, the Council has this to say: 'This love is uniquely expressed and perfected through the marital act. The actions in marriage by which the couple are united intimately and chastely are noble and worthy ones. Expressed in a manner which is truly human, these actions signify and promote the mutual self giving by which spouses enrich each other with a joyful and thankful will' (Pastoral Constitution Part 2, chapter 1).

In an Anglican statement, *Marriage and the Church's Task*,[9] we find 'this polyphony of love finds expression in the lovers' bodily union. This is not to be comprehended simply in terms of two individuals' experience of ecstatic pleasure. Such it certainly may be, but it is always more. It is an act of personal commitment that spans past, present and future. It is celebration, healing, renewed pledge and promise. Sexual intercourse can "mean" many different things to husband and wife, according to mood and circumstance. Above all, it communicates the affirmation of mutual belonging.' These Anglican and Roman Catholic views were reinforced by the 1980 Methodist report, *A Christian Understanding of Human Sexuality*,[10] which focuses on the joy of sexual love. 'Sexual love, including genital acts when they express that love, shares in the divine act of loving with every human activity which is creative, dedicated and generous. Yet until recently Western Christian attitudes have shown little enthusiasm for the idea of sexual love as an element of Christian living. . . .' (Article 28). 'Despite the biblical references to the joy which God gives to his children, most Western traditional

Christian attitudes have not accepted enjoyment as an essential part of God's design for mankind. Physical pleasures have been frequently equated with sin. Since sexuality provides some of the greatest pleasures, it has therefore been most suspect. This rejection of joy warps the Christian understanding of the love of God, the goodness of his creation and the wholeness of human nature . . . Sexuality is not merely useful. It is enjoyable, purposeful and fulfilling. It is a means whereby man and woman may glorify God and grow in the fulfilment of one another' (Article 29).

The Church of Scotland in its second report to the General Assembly, entitled *Human Sexuality*,[11] comes to the significant conclusion that sexuality serves primarily to initiate, cement and enrich relationships. Procreation is a 'second order' function of sexuality, ordained of God but not its main role, which is to do with relationship.

Father Kelly concludes that the Churches are veering towards the view that human sexuality is primarily to be seen in its relational significance. This is not necessarily or essentially bound up with procreative function, and the quality of relationship 'is the prime criterion of sexual ethics'. This 'quality of relationship' is intimately linked with love. Several of the main reports from the Churches in the last 40 years have referred to this love and its creative potential.

This inner world of sexual intercourse has not been analysed in any detail and so Christianity, having moved from seeing sex primarily in terms of procreation to seeing it in terms of relationship, has no real basis for an alternative to casual sex. References to love have no persuasive authority because love is such a difficult word to understand and yet, ultimately, all human behaviour in Christianity is based on the fundamental teaching of Jesus that all commandments are subordinate to the ones of loving God and loving one's neighbour as oneself. There is no question that the meaning of sexuality is to be found in love, and this book is dedicated to analysing what we mean by love in sexual human relationships.

Part II

The Inner Meaning
of Sexual Intercourse

Chapter 6

Sexuality in Childhood

For many, adult sexuality is the only form known and understood. The child is considered to be asexual. This is not the case and in this chapter we will review the physical and psychological basis of sexuality in childhood. We begin with the physical. The most basic manifestation of our sexuality lies in our chromosomes, which are present in every cell of the body. The normal female has two XX chromosomes, the male has one X and one Y, the latter determining maleness. The foetus has a primitive medulla and a cortex. In the presence of the somatic male-determining factor, the medulla develops into a testes and the cortex regresses. In the absence of a male factor, the cortex develops into an ovary. The testes start to produce testosterone from about the eighth week of pregnancy onwards. In addition to the testes and the ovary, the foetus produces the external genitalia of a penis and the associated male organs and in the female it develops a vagina, uterus and fallopian tubes. In the male, the penis and the testicles are visible and give the boy external signs with which to identify its maleness. The girl has no such external characteristics. Thus throughout life sexual arousal which is expressed in the male with an erect penis is a more complex phenomenon in the female. In the brain, the original status is female and in the male this is overridden with androgenic male hormones.

Given the biological factors, when does gender assume a fixed character? Stoller[1] called this the core gender identity, when 'I am male' or 'I am female' become fixed. This stage is reached between the age of two to three years. This critical period has interested psychologists with respect to incorrect gender assignment and the possibility of correction. Diamond[2] suggests that correction can be made as late as 13 or 14 years of age. It can be seen that disorders of gender and sexual identity can occur as a result of physical development or hormonal malfunctioning. These do not concern us in this book, but details are to be found in an excellent text book by Bancroft.[3]

Society and Christianity have been so obsessed with masturbation and sex play, towards which they have shown concern and disgust, that they have failed to appreciate that both are common from early infancy. Galenson and Roiple[4] observed young children in a nursery and found that boys began genital play at about six to seven months of age, whereas girls start at ten to eleven months. They found that boys continued this play until more obvious masturbation starts at 15 to 16 months. Masturbation to the point of orgasm is observed in both sexes as young as six months. Behaviour of this kind is reported by parents at these very young ages and will continue unashamed if adults do not discourage it. It is clear from this evidence that the anxiety felt by millions of Christians for a long time is the product of culture, and that the sexual guilt experienced by adults starts very early in childhood.

The average age for a slightly more adult form of masturbation is about eight to nine years for boys, and a little earlier for girls. Associated with masturbation is the orgasm. Before puberty, without male ejaculation, the adult significance is not appreciated by either sex, but the consensus is that it does occur. In the findings of Kinsey,[5] the authors came to the conclusion that, in an uninhibited society, more than half of the boys would experience orgasm by the age of three to four years, and nearly all within three to four years prior to puberty. Something similar pertains for girls.

Erections in the male are similarly recorded from a very early age and continue throughout childhood. So that masturbation, with erection in the male, leading to orgasm, is a well-established experience in childhood. At puberty there are well-known secondary characteristics in both girls and boys. These physical manifestations at puberty herald a stage in sexual development when the child turns away from the parents and veers usually to a person of the opposite sex. A small number have a proclivity for their own sex. This phase marks the incest taboo, when children cross the threshold to adulthood and the long journey to courtship and marriage begins.

The subject of sexual abuse is extensive and only the merest outline will be mentioned here. Sexual abuse occurs when a child is used by an adult for sexual purposes. Both boys and girls can be abused, but the latter are more commonly assaulted. Sexual abuse ranges from sexual penetration to fondling and sometimes the girl is asked to masturbate the male. Undressing the child may be involved. All this often takes place within the family, and frequently step-parents may be involved. The child is often frightened and keeps the experience hidden from other adults. In the process, the child is anxious and guilty about sex and moves on to adulthood traumatised. Sexual abuse in childhood, as we are finding nowadays, is common, and adults may enter their own sexual relationships with problems from sexual experiences that they carry from their childhood. The worst effect is a disjunction between love and sex and it takes a lot of patient loving in marriage for the wound to heal.

After puberty adolescents enter the world of sexual friendship, courtship, cohabitation and marriage. The details of this phase will be considered in subsequent chapters. The physical sexual development of childhood proceeds usually in an undisturbed, spontaneous way and, except for a few abnormalities of a physical and hormonal nature, allows growth to take place uninterruptedly to puberty. Whilst the physical growth takes place, the child is learning about sex from what it sees in the behaviour of its parents and other adults. In other words it is a time of intense social learning. Parents may convey sexual education by assuaging the curiosity of their children when a younger sibling arrives, but the greatest impact on a child is what it sees and hears from its parents. In addition parents play a vital role in how they approach genital play and masturbation in their children. They can give the child a sense of joy and approval of their bodies and experimentation, or a sense of anxiety and disgust. The anxieties of the adults are communicated to the child, and what we learn in the first dozen years of life plays a vital role in our adult sexual feelings. In particular, parents become pre-occupied with their adolescent children's sexual behaviour. It is important to realise that how adults behave is greatly influenced by their education pre-pubertally and parents have a grave responsibility to communicate a positive, joyful association in early childhood.

Both the physical and psychological dimensions of childhood sexuality take us away from the belief in childhood sexual innocence. Parents have for a long time held on to the conviction that there is no sexuality in childhood and that it only commences with puberty, an utterly mistaken view. The man who exploded this myth was Sigmund Freud. He identified a childhood sexuality other than genital play. In the course of his psychoanalytic work, he postulated that the human personality develops from two basic drives of sexuality and aggression. As far as sexuality is concerned, he located its roots in the physical sensations derived from the smooth lining (mucus membrane) of the mouth, the anus and the genitals. He suggested that the earliest sensual experiences were located in the mouth, lips and tongue and were activated in the first year in the oral phase. Thus breastfeeding came to play such an important role in dynamic theory. The first experiences of love are to be found in the interaction between mother and child, and satiation or a good feed plays a vital role in the sense of fulfilment of the baby. This oral phase, dependent on the stimulation of the mucus membrane of the mouth, remains sexually important throughout life. The mouth is the site of kissing and this is a vital sexual display.

Feeding for the baby is a form of receptivity, taking in, or in more technical terms 'internalisation'. When we love somebody, we often say, 'I would like to eat you.' It is the earliest experience of bringing another person inside us and we go on internalising those we love for the rest of our lives. We not only take in food (milk) but we spit it out or, in psychological terms, reject it. We do the same with people. We take them in our psyche and we may reject them. The subtle balance of accepting and rejecting human beings in relationships begins in this oral phase of taking in and spitting out food.

With the arrival of teeth, the baby is introduced to biting and the aggressive mode. Now the pleasure of swallowing is intermingled with the satisfaction of biting. The passive is now mixed with the active and the roots of sado-masochism are instituted. All this may sound far-fetched, but what Freud described are real experiences in the baby and they leave an enduring mark in the personality.

All this happens in the first year of life. In my book *One Like Us*[6] I describe the common dynamic theories current at present. There I indicated that Melanie Klein, an early follower of Freud, who worked with children, postulated that the breast was the site of an intense drama for the baby. A hungry baby sucks at the breast, is satiated and feels good. This gives it a good experience of feeling loved. If the baby feels hungry, sucks at the breast and finds no milk, then it gets angry, aggressive and, in fantasy, chews the breast to bits. For the baby, the breast stands for the whole mother and Klein postulated the beginnings of personal aggression in this biting, tearing experience. Thus love and hate begin in this early phase of development. All these events are postulated because it is very difficult to enter the psyche of a one-year-old baby. But it is not hard to imagine the battle of love and hate over food that are certainly observable in the older child. Another characteristic of the first year of life is the intimacy of touch between baby and parent. The manner of holding the baby lays the foundations, according to Erikson, of a sense of trust. It is not difficult to visualise that the sense of trust, which is so vital in a sexual exchange, begins so early in life. Lovers who have sexual intercourse are entirely at each other's mercy during the act. Trust is a vital component of relationship and it is not difficult to perceive that the roots of this trust begin at the very start of life. The whole exchange of courtship leading to intercourse is a process of building mutual trust in which physical security is central to the experience. This physical security is learnt in the arms and on the knees of our parents.

Winnicott goes further and suggests that not only does trust develop in the exchange of holding and being held, but also the quality of the holding is a contribution to feeling loved. Certainly in adult life we can distinguish between gentle and rough handling, and we interpret the difference in terms of love. Once again the roots of this love are learnt in early childhood.

Thus the first year of life is the origin of stimulation at the mouth, love and hate experiences, trust, touch, love and security. The way the baby is handled leaves an enduring experience on its interpersonal signals of love.

As we move to the second and third year of life, Freud postulated that the child becomes aware of the other end of the gastrointestinal canal. The focus is now on the anus that is also lined with mucous membrane and, when stimulated, gives pleasurable experiences. Just as the oral phase is linked with the pleasure of taking in and spitting out or rejecting, so the anal phase is associated with retention and expulsion. The anal phase of libidinal development leaves its mark in a variety of ways. Some people are preoccupied with cleanliness and their bowels, and get sexually excited when the anus is stimulated. The anus may be stimulated with enemas, or penetrated with the penis or other objects. In all these situations, sexual pleasure may be derived. In our society we have mixed feelings about bowel action and the accompanying sensual stimulation.

Erikson describes the second and third year of life as a phase of autonomy. All parents can see the battle between the independence acquired by the toddler learning to walk, dress, eat and talk, and the dependence of finding these processes difficult and turning to the parents for help. This battle continues throughout life and lovers are not immune from a relationship in which they display these characteristics towards each other.

Finally, Freud reached the age of four and five, when the famous Oedipus and Electra complexes are worked out. In the Oedipus complex, the boy feels attracted to the mother and it is only the imaginary threat of castration by the father that pushes him to move away from his mother towards the father, identifying with him. The opposite takes place with the girl in the Electra complex. For Freudians, the resolution of the Oedipus and Electra complexes is vital for adult sexual maturity. In life we find men who are still attached to their mothers and girls to their fathers and who find it difficult to form an attachment with a person of the opposite sex. Whether this is due to the principle stated by Freud or to other reasons is not always clear.

The works of Freud, Melanie Klein, Winnicott and Erikson are all based on Freudian libido theory. An exception to this was provided by John Bowlby, also considered in *One Like Us*, a British psychoanalyst who postulated that the bond between child and mother was not sexual and based on food, but on an evolutionary basis of human attachment and bonding. Basing his theory on ethology, the study of bonds shown by animals attaching themselves to their parents, he suggested that the infant forms an affective attachment to its mother through vision, by recognising her face and then the rest of her body; through sound, by recognising her voice; touch, by holding and being held; and smell. Through these dimensions the child forms a link with its mother, who becomes a secure base. From this secure base the child explores the world around it and, when frightened or anxious, returns to her for security. The observation of any child will give credence to this theory. Bowlby maintained that attachment behaviour characterises human beings from the cradle to the grave. From the point of view of this book, the subjective experience of falling in love is a form of attachment behaviour. Below I shall trace the similarities between the infant care giver and the baby and adult lovers as given by Shaver, Hazan and Bradshaw.[7] The formation and quality of the attachment bond between carers and baby depends on the baby's sensitivity and responsiveness. Adult love feelings are related to an intense desire for the lover's interest and reciprocation.

- The mother provides a secure base and the baby feels competent and safe to explore. Lovers' real or imagined reciprocation causes a person to feel confident, secure and safe.
- When the mother (in all instances, the mother can be substituted by father or another adult) is present, the baby is happier and less afraid of strangers. When the lover is viewed as responding, he or she is happier, more positive about life in general, more outgoing and kinder to others.
- When the mother is not available or not sensitive, the baby is anxious and preoccupied. When the lover is uninterested or rejecting, the beloved is anxious, preoccupied and unable to concentrate.
- Bonding includes proximity, contact seeking, holding, touching, caressing, kissing, rocking, smiling, following and clinging. Romantic love is manifested in wanting to spend time with the loved one, holding, touching, caressing, kissing and making love.
- When afraid, distressed, sick or threatened, the baby seeks physical contact with its mother. When afraid, distressed, sick or threatened, lovers like to be held and comforted by their partner.
- Distress at separation or loss leads to crying, calling for the

mother, trying to find her, becoming sad and listless if reunion is impossible. Distress at separation or loss, crying, calling for the loved one, trying to find them, and becoming sad and listless are the hallmarks of adult separation.

- Upon reunion the baby smiles, greets its mother with shouts of joy and wants to be picked up. Upon return, lovers rejoice, become ecstatic and rejoice.
- The baby shares its things and toys with its mother. Lovers like to share experiences and gifts with one another.
- The baby engages in prolonged eye contact and is fascinated by the physical features of the mother. Lovers frequently engage in prolonged eye contact, are fascinated by each other's bodily features and like to explore them.
- The baby has a balance of closeness and distance with the mother. Lovers have a balance of physical and emotional distance with each other.
- Although the baby can be attached to more than one person, there is usually a key attachment that is often the mother. Whilst adults feel that they can love more than one person, intense love tends to occur with only one partner at a time.
- The baby coos, 'sings', utters baby talk and its mother responds in the same style. Lovers too coo, sing, exchange baby talk, use soft tones to one another and there is much communication which is non-verbal.
- The responsive mother senses the infant's needs and has a powerful empathy with it. Lovers feel equally powerfully understood and empathised with.
- The baby gets tremendous pleasure from its mother's approval, approbation and attention. Lovers, particularly in the early stages of the relationship, get tremendous happiness from each other's approval.

This long list is persuasive that attachment behaviour in childhood is very similar to falling in love and courtship in adulthood. It is given here as the most powerful example of experiences in childhood which are repeated when falling in love in adulthood.

Cognitive psychology would say that all the approbation and disapproval that comes into play in adulthood can be explained by adult cognition. This does not explain why we respond to certain cues, for example smiles, kissing, touch and the whole repertoire of courtship, unless we were sensitised in childhood to its bonding meaning.

Bowlby himself had no doubt that, in terms of subjective experience, the formation of a bond is described as 'falling in love', maintaining a bond as 'loving someone' and losing a partner as 'grieving over someone'. This model of attachment behaviour as the equivalent of falling in love is very powerful and is offered as our main psychological understanding of the prelude to sexual intercourse. Bowlby not only described attachment behaviour but also detachment or separation. Detachment explains why some relationships fade away over time because the affective bond loses its affectivity and one-time lovers become strangers in a subsequent period.

Attachment theory also explains the frequent falling in love experiences of adolescence. One of the key essentials of human behaviour is the ability to identify the permanent falling in love encounter from the transient ones in which the affective gradually disappears over time. The former is the setting for permanency and sexual intercourse, the latter is inappropriate for coitus. We have not yet learnt to distinguish clearly between the two experiences, and believing too early that this encounter is the real one leads to premature intercourse and possibly to a pregnancy that is not based on an enduring relationship. We shall consider these matters in the next chapter.

Chapter 7

Adolescent Sexuality

One of the myths perpetrated in the whole of society – but especially in the Christian community – is that the first experience of sexual intercourse takes place after marriage, a view held particularly by the older generation because for many of them, especially women, it was true. It is certainly no longer true. During the last 40 years, young people have engaged in sexual intercourse at a steadily earlier period. Before sexual intercourse, there is an anticipatory time of dating behaviour. The onset of dating behaviour appears to be related to age rather than to the onset of puberty.[1] In an extensive study of young West German adolescents,[2] sexual behaviour was found to unfold from social dating to kissing, petting and sexual intercourse. By the age of 11, 69 % of boys and 55 % of girls had had at least one date, and 56 % of boys and 47 % of girls had kissed a member of the opposite sex. By the age of 11, 25 % of boys and 12 % of girls had experienced heavy petting, but none had had sexual intercourse. But by the age of 13, 31 % of boys and 21 % of girls had had coitus. While social and biological factors play a part in initiating intercourse, in a study of 102 boys of eighth, ninth and tenth grade,[3] the hormone testosterone was found to be the most powerful relator to sexual activity. It would appear, therefore, that in adolescent boys, biologically active testosterone is more important in starting erotic behaviour than social factors. For girls, the opposite is true. The main reason why a girl engages in sexual behaviour is not hormonal, but due to peer group pressure.

Mention has been made of the sixties as the starting point from which sexual intercourse increased in young people. A key study, *Sexual Behaviour in Britain*[4], states that for women born between

1931 and 1935, the median age at first sexual intercourse was 21 years. Thereafter it steadily declines. The median age at first intercourse for those born between 1966 and 1975 was 17. The dramatic reduction of age at first sexual intercourse is matched with a drop in age of first sexual experience. At the time of the publication of this study, 1994, men aged 16 to 24 had their first sexual experience at the age of 13, and first intercourse at 17. Women had respective ages of 14 and 17. The above are median ages. The figures are given also for those who had sexual intercourse below the age of 16. For those interviewed who were aged between 16 and 19, 18 % of women and 27.6 % of men had had sexual intercourse. Sometimes even higher instances are quoted. Even these conservative estimates suggest that in the youngest age groups, nearly 1 in 5 of girls and 1 in 3 of boys have had sexual intercourse by the age of 16. The median age of first sexual intercourse is higher in social class 1, three years later for men, than in social class 5. The same difference is found for women.

As far as the age of partner at first intercourse is concerned, men's partners tend to be roughly the same age as themselves. This applies also to those who are under the age of 16. Two thirds of men aged under 16 at first intercourse had partners who were also under the age of 16. For women the pattern is different. An older partner at first intercourse is the norm. Of women aged 13–17, 75 % at first intercourse had partners older than themselves.

While there is a great increase of sexual intercourse in adolescence, it is not casual. For those who had sexual intercourse before the age of 16, the partner was known but not in a steady relationship for 42 % of men and 28 % of women, but was in a steady relationship for 35 % of men and nearly 60 % of women. It is uncommon, in fact rare, for the first intercourse to take place within marriage. The morality of sexual intercourse in this age group will be discussed in Chapter 14.

How do youngsters feel about having sexual intercourse before the age of 16? The study showed that about 25 % of men and 60 % of women felt they had sexual intercourse too soon, and 73 % of men and 40 % of women considered that they had it at about the right time. The higher proportion of girls who regretted their early experiences shows how social pressure is an important factor in having intercourse before girls are psychologically ready for it. This points to the huge need for education in this area. The main reason given for having sexual intercourse under the age of 16 was curiosity in 40 % of men and 23 % of women; 6 % of men and 40 % of women claimed to be in love. This is a marked difference for the sexes and it shows that romantic factors play a much greater role for girls under the age of 16 than they do for boys. This links with the psychological theory of psychological attachment discussed in the previous chapter.

Thus the increase of sexual activity in teenagers is marked and it has consequences for teenage pregnancies and infection if contraception is not used. A recent study[5] shows that between a third and a half of sexually active teenagers do not use contraception at first intercourse, a much higher proportion than in many other European countries. It is not surprising, therefore, that there is both a high rate of sexually transmitted diseases and pregnancy. The study shows that the live birth rate for women aged 15–19 per thousand women is nearly 23. This is the highest teenage birth rate in Western Europe, with higher rates only in Canada, New Zealand and the United States.

In 1997 in England 90,000 teenagers became pregnant, resulting in 56,000 live births. Nearly 7,700 conceptions were to girls under the age of 16, resulting in 3,700 births. 2,200 conceptions were to girls aged 14 and under. Around 15 % of conceptions under 16 ended in abortion.

The risk of teenage pregnancy is greatest for young people who have grown up in poverty and are disadvantaged, or for those with poor educational attainment. Overall, teenage parenthood is more common in areas of deprivation and poverty, but even the most prosperous areas have higher rates of teenage births than the average in some comparable European countries. In this chapter I have outlined the facts about youthful sexuality. They reflect historic social changes in sexual behaviour and offer a challenge to the Christian community. This challenge will be considered in Chapter 26. It is a challenge in sexual knowledge, education, the use of contraception and morality.

Chapter 8

Sexual Attraction and Adult Intercourse

By the late teens most young men and women are sexually active and the overwhelming majority of young adults are in a relationship of cohabitation or marriage. In this and the next five chapters (which are the central focus of the book), the inner world of sexual intercourse will be considered.

Sexual attraction

As a prelude to sexual intercourse, there is sexual desire. Sexual desire has been attacked, condemned, associated with sin and, even to this day, there are those who, through a negative religious upbringing, are afraid to trust their senses and enjoy the erotic. Yet we have to look no further than Scripture itself for an exaltation of the human body. Hardly in a place of pre-eminence, the Song of Songs has straddled time to teach us that in the body and the erotic are to be found a divine plan of the goodness of creation.

We are inundated nowadays with sexual pictures and scenes in the media, but all of them have been anticipated in the Song of Songs. Its contents are poems describing the sexual fervour between a young man and a woman. The rich language tells us that sexual attraction and desire have not changed over the ages. The Song opens with a passage from the girl:

> Let him kiss me with the kisses of his mouth.
> Your love is more delightful than wine;

delicate is the fragrance of your perfume,
your name is an oil poured out,
and that is why the maidens love you.
Draw me in your footsteps, let us run.
The King has brought me into his rooms;
you will be our joy and our gladness.
We shall praise your love above wine;
how right it is to love you.

Tell me then, you whom my heart loves:
Where will you lead your flock to graze,
where will you rest it at noon?
That I may no more wander like a vagabond
beside the flocks of your companions.
If you do not know this, O loveliest of women,
follow the tracks of the flock,
and take your kids to graze close by the shepherds' tents.

We shall make you golden earrings
and beads of silver.
While the King rests in his own room
my nard yields its perfume.
My Beloved is a sachet of myrrh
lying between my breasts.
My Beloved is a cluster of henna flowers
among the vines of Engedi.

(S. of S. 1:1–4, 7, 11–14)

A brief description of the girl's skin colour follows. When one thinks of the millions of pounds spent today in order to achieve a tan, in those days the woman considered it a possible hindrance to her attractiveness:

I am black but lovely, daughters of Jerusalem,
like the tents of Kedar,
like the pavilion of Salmah.
Take no notice of my swarthiness,
it is the sun that has burnt me.
My mother's sons turned their anger on me,

they made me look after the vineyards.
Had I only looked after my own!
                    (S. of S. 1:5–6)

In turn the man, named as lover, compares the girl whom he calls
his love to his house:

To my mare harnessed to Pharaoh's chariot
I compare you, my love.
Your cheeks show fair between their pendants
and your neck within its necklaces.
                    (S. of S. 1:9–10)

How beautiful you are, my Beloved,
and how delightful!
All green is our bed.
                    (S. of S. 1:16)

There follows the idealisation of the girl:

As a lily among the thistles,
so is my love among the maidens.
                    (S. of S. 2:2)

Physical intimacy is expressed by the girl:

His left arm is under my head,
his right embraces me.
                    (S. of S. 2:6)

The adoration by the man continues in the second poem. He calls
her a dove:

My dove, hiding in the clefts of the rock,
in the coverts of the cliff,
show me your face,
let me hear your voice;
for your voice is sweet
and your face is beautiful.
                    (S. of S. 2:14)

John Bowlby who, in the description of attachment of the baby to
the mother extended this theory to falling in love, shows us how

vision and sound are crucial to attraction. Here we see both high-lighted. Further still, the man extols the beauty of the girl:

> How beautiful you are, my love,
> how beautiful you are!
> Your eyes,
> behind your veil, are doves;
> your hair is like a flock of goats
> surging down the slopes of Gilead.
> Your teeth are like a flock of shorn ewes
> as they come up from the washing.
> Each one has its twin,
> not one unpaired with another.
> Your lips are a scarlet thread
> and your words enchanting.
> Your cheeks, behind your veil,
> are halves of pomegranate.
> Your neck is the Tower of David
> built as a fortress,
> hung round with a thousand bucklers,
> and each the shield of a hero.
> Your two breasts are two fawns,
> twins of a gazelle,
> that feed among the lilies.
>
> (S. of S. 4:1–5)

If we make allowances for a different cultural setting, here is a description of feminine beauty that has stood the test of time, and it elicits sexual desire:

> You ravish my heart,
> my sister, my promised bride,
> you ravish my heart
> with a single one of your glances,
> with one single pearl of your necklace.
>
> (S. of S. 4:9)

This sexual desire is experienced as a sickness of love and we find this echoed in 'that I am sick with love' (S. of S. 5:8).

Having had a description of the woman by the man, we now have
that of the man by the woman:

> My Beloved is fresh and ruddy,
> to be known among ten thousand.
> His head is golden, purest gold,
> his locks are palm fronds
> and black as the raven.
> His eyes are like doves
> at a pool of water,
> bathed in milk,
> at rest on a pool.
> His cheeks are beds of spices,
> banks sweetly scented.
> His lips are lilies,
> distilling pure myrrh.
> His hands are golden, rounded,
> set with jewels of Tarshish.
> His belly a block of ivory
> covered with sapphires.
> His legs are alabaster columns
> set in sockets of pure gold.
> His appearance is that of Lebanon,
> unrivalled as the cedars.
> His conversation is sweetness itself,
> he is altogether lovable.
> Such is my Beloved, such is my friend,
> O daughters of Jerusalem.
>
> (S. of S. 5:10–16)

In the presence of such intense physical attraction, its quality is
translated into love. She says:

> I am my Beloved's, and my Beloved is mine.
> He pastures his flock among the lilies.
>
> (S. of S. 6:3)

This sense of mutual belonging, expressed by all lovers, is given in
one sentence and there is still further articulation of her physical
beauty:

How beautiful are your feet in their sandals,
O prince's daughter!
The curve of your thighs is like the curve of a necklace,
work of a master hand.
Your navel is a bowl well rounded
with no lack of wine,
your belly a heap of wheat
surrounded with lilies.
Your two breasts are two fawns,
twins of a gazelle.
Your neck is an ivory tower.
Your eyes, the pools of Heshbon,
by the gate of Bath-rabbim.
Your nose, the Tower of Lebanon,
sentinel facing Damascus.

(S. of S. 7:2–5)

Beauty invites the desire of touch. The man wants to touch her breasts:

How beautiful you are, how charming,
my love, my delight!
In stature like the palm tree,
its fruit-clusters your breasts.
'I will climb the palm tree,' I resolved,
'I will seize its cluster of dates!'
May your breasts be clusters of grapes,
your breath sweet-scented as apples,
your speaking superlative wine.

(S. of S. 7:7–9)

The girl knows she is desired:

I am my Beloved's,
and his desire is for me.

(S. of S. 7:11)

And this intense mutual desire is expressed in language for ever on the lips of lovers:

Set me like a seal on your heart,
like a seal on your arm.

58

For love is strong as Death,
jealousy relentless as Sheol.
The flash of it is a flash of fire,
a flame of Yahweh himself.
Love no flood can quench,
no torrents drown.
Were a man to offer all the wealth of his house
to buy love,
contempt is all he would gain.

(S. of S. 8:6–7)

Despite the intense preoccupation with the erotic in our day, it is doubtful whether sexual attraction and desire have ever been depicted with such beauty and intensity. The central point of this poem is that all these feelings are situated at the heart of God, Yahweh himself. Sexual attraction has a divine flame and the ardour that burns in the hearts of boys and girls, men and women, links that love with the very essence of the divine.

A previous generation of Christians, particularly Catholics, were preoccupied with how far couples could go in visualising and touching the erotic in the body. The body was a zone of 'no go' areas and guilt saturated the minds of couples whose natural desire was the riches of the senses. That preoccupation with sexual sins and their confession denied the beauty of the work of God.

Falling in love

The sexual attraction and desire delicately portrayed in the Song of Songs is the prelude of love for sexual intercourse itself. Nevertheless we are physically attracted by many people, but in general we want to make love to one person. What makes the difference? Falling in love is a complex experience, which we do not quite understand. In her book *Falling in Love*[1] Sheila Sullivan says, 'There is no monolithic explanation for love and little agreement on what actually happens. The vast majority of people, who believe that falling in love is a genuine, palpable event, know that its essentials include sexual excitement, obsession, intimacy, idealisation, fantasy, an urge

59

to commitment and (in an elementary form of "merging") the creation of a new entity: "we".'

In this book we shall confine ourselves to what has been established scientifically as having the greatest contribution to falling in love, as we are primarily concerned with sexual intercourse itself. We have established that sexual attraction is a prominent part of love and have illustrated it with quotations from the Song of Songs. Next I refer to the psychodynamic theories of falling in love and in particular to Bowlby's theory of attachment that in my opinion is very important. Briefly, as discussed in Chapter 6, Bowlby states that the infant forms an emotional attachment with mother, then with father and later with other figures, based on the attraction of vision, sound, touch and smell. In this way it forms an affectionate bond. Bowlby believed that we have a capacity to form affective bonds from cradle to grave. For him, falling in love and the behaviours of lovers is the formation of an affective bond in which the couple want to be together, enjoy each other's company, idealise their characteristics, feel secure in their attachment, and get a great deal of pleasure from looks, touch and holding one another. Thus, in so far as we can unravel the mystery of falling in love, I am postulating the presence of sexual attraction within which an affective bond is formed and the man and woman form a couple, a relationship which they want to consummate. Biologically, in evolutionary terms, this consummation is designed for procreation, but the immediate experiences that set the process in motion are sexual excitation and the formation of a bond. Within these two parameters lie the prelude to intercourse itself.

Sexual intercourse

Heterosexual sexual intercourse is a universal experience that will be briefly outlined here. Its detailed study is of recent origin and its most accurate description is that of Masters and Johnson.[2] Masters and Johnson describe four phases of intercourse: the excitement phase, the plateau, the orgasm and the resolution phase. Given that a man and woman have found each other emotionally pleasing enough to form an attachment and sexually exciting enough to desire each other, they proceed to the excitement phase.

The first sign of sexual arousal in a man is of course the erection of the penis, failure of which leads to impotence. This erection of the penis is due either to erotic arousal or to manual stimulation. Without going into the details, the anatomy of this organ is so structured that, in the presence of sexual excitement, blood rushes into it, engorging it and giving it a stiff erection.

As far as women are concerned, the first sign of excitation is the moistening of the vagina with a lubricating fluid. As with the erection of the penis, this lubrication occurs either as a result of stimulation of the woman's genital region, of her breasts or with erotic arousal. This vaginal lubrication is due to a sweating reaction occurring in the walls of the vagina. This sweating of the vagina is the earliest stage of women's readiness for intercourse and of the lubrication that eases the entry of the penis into the vagina.

There is however more to female sexual response than the sweating of the vaginal walls. Important changes occur in the clitoris. This organ is situated just above the entrance of the vagina. The clitoris is full of sensitive nerve endings whose stimulation contributes to the erotic, pleasurable response of the woman. In the excitation state the nipples of the breast undergo erection, and the breasts increase in size. In addition to the changes in both partners, the entire body participates in the excitement phase. The muscles tense up, the pulse rate speeds up, blood pressure rises and a 'sex flush' appears in the skin.

The next phase of intercourse coincides with the entry of the penis into the vagina and is called the plateau. Within this plateau phase there is an acceleration of breathing and of the pulse rate and blood pressure. Muscles tense up. The thrusting of the penis to and fro in the vagina gives an exquisite pleasure to its shaft and to the vagina in the woman. In the woman there is formed an 'orgasmic platform' which is an engorgement and swelling of tissue surrounding the outer third of the vagina. As a result of this swelling, the diameter is reduced and this gives a stronger grip to the penis. During this phase there is mounting excitation in both men and women due to the engorgement of blood vessels and other organs, and an increase in muscle tension. Both men and woman are now ready for orgasm.

The major event of orgasm in the man is the ejaculation of semen accompanied by an intense pleasure in the presence of the rhythmic spasms of the ejaculation. In the female, orgasm is also a series of rhythmic contractions of the orgasmic platform. These contractions are muscular in character. A mild female orgasm may be accompanied by three to five contractions, and a powerful one by eight to twelve.

In both sexes the events in the genitals are accompanied by changes in the rest of the body. Pulse rate, breathing and blood pressure reach a peak. The sexual flush is pronounced and muscles contract.

The orgasm is the key moment in intercourse and, although brief in time, is monumental in significance. It initiates the release of the muscular tension throughout the body and the withdrawal of blood in the engorged blood vessels. In the final phase, the resolution is marked by changes in the woman which include the clitoris returning to its original position, the orgasmic platform relaxing and the vagina shrinking. It may take half an hour before the female body returns to its original, unstimulated state. In men, the most obvious sign is the loss of erection and the shrinkage of the penis. In both men and women the pulse rate, blood pressure and the breathing return to normal. For the man there is a refractory phase in which he cannot get sexually excited again. In young people this period is brief, as short as ten minutes, but as men age it takes a longer time. Women do not have a refractory period and many women, if stimulated again, can have a further orgasm.

Moral issues

Sexual intercourse has been studied most intensely in marriage. The concern of this book is with those links that have traditionally aroused moral hostility. The first of these is the position for intercourse. Before the modern scientific period, it used to be believed that the position taken by the couple influenced the capacity to enhance the possibility of procreation. In particular, it was believed that the man on top of the woman facilitated new life. We now know that position does not matter and couples may choose, with total moral impunity, whatever position they like.

Another moral dimension is the orifice that the penis enters.

Traditionally, when the main purpose of sexual intercourse was procreation, only vaginal intercourse was considered moral. But as we shall see in the course of the book, procreation is neither the primary nor principal reason for coitus. Its principal reason is its enhancement of love, which in turn reflects divine love and the nature of God. Thus couples, within the dictates of the law of the country in which they live, may have intercourse any way they want. But vaginal intercourse remains the most usual for it is emotionally and physiologically most suited to generate the pleasurable and procreative response for which intercourse is designed.

Beyond position and orifices used, there exists the world of sexual variations, that is to say additional sexual excitation from practices, behaviours and fetishes (sexual arousal objects) that provoke sexual arousal beyond the normal visual, auditory and touch sources. Thus sadomasochist practices, the wearing of rubber, leather or certain clothing, the importance of the foot as a fetish – and indeed anything – may become a substitute for sexual arousal. The Christian world is silent about these practices. They have not been considered suitable subjects for discussion, presumably because they enhance sexual pleasure, which has been a taboo subject. The fact is that men and women, particularly the former, may be aroused by a whole variety of situations. Provided they are mutually acceptable, are not demeaning or humiliating and do not cause unacceptable pain, they are perfectly moral and legitimate to employ.

We have now briefly outlined the setting for falling in love, which leads to sexual intercourse with its pinnacle, the orgasm. But is the orgasm the only value to be derived from coitus? Is pleasure the only reward or, as it was considered for centuries, is the reward procreation? For the whole of Christianity, procreation has been seen as the main purpose of intercourse. This approach has reduced coitus to biology and until recent times it was this limited understanding of the act which gave rise to the moral considerations of its meaning. In this sense for nearly all of its history Christianity diminished the value of coitus and could not see beyond procreation, which is not to say that procreation is unimportant. But as we have seen in the examination of coitus itself, its biological end is invariably the orgasm, not procreation. Only rarely is fertilisation the end result. Is the orgasm itself the end of the story?

Christianity, afraid of sexual pleasure and unwilling to allocate it a divine meaning, as in the Song of Songs, could only take refuge in procreation, which is an obvious purpose. But is orgasm and its association with occasional procreation the ultimate goal of sexual intercourse? Although the orgasm is clearly the end result of intercourse, in my opinion it is not its ultimate meaning.

Sexual intercourse is an encounter between persons and its ultimate meaning is interpersonal. In the chapters that follow I shall describe this meaning in terms of a language, in which the couples are speaking to and communicating with each other with their bodies. This is a communication of love. It is a language that shifts the individual from egoism to a mutuality of sharing. They are sharing each other. It is a language that shifts the technology of pleasure to mutual commitment. And finally, it is a shift from potentially meaningless pleasure to meaningful interaction. Thus the physical becomes a channel of communication for the personal. This personal communication develops over time. As the couple move from being in love to loving, and as the loving changes with time, so sexual intercourse speaks a different language.

The idea that, in sexual intercourse, persons and not just bodies communicate, and that they do so in a language of love, arises for me from the roots of human growth. The baby is held, stroked, caressed and kissed – all physical experiences which, before the advent of language, to the child convey love. The growing person is accustomed to communicate with the body, and sexuality concluding in sexual intercourse is a way of transmitting the personal history and details of one's life. John Paul II claims in his *The Theology of the Body*, 'that in sexual donation the couple indeed speak a "language of the body", expressing in a manner more profound than words the totality of the gift to each other.'[3]

In *The Body in Context*,[4] Gareth Moore refers to the work of the Pope and myself and critically assesses it. His book is written in a philosophical context but expresses the same ideas as here. In general there is a slow but gradual development of sexuality as personal communication. In the next few chapters I explore these thoughts further.

Chapter 9

Sexual Intercourse and Personal Love

As I said in the previous chapter, the natural consequence of sexual attraction and falling in love is intercourse with the pinnacle of the orgasm. It would be utterly inconsistent with what we know of human beings if the biology of the orgasm was the end of the road. Couples do not say to one another, 'Let's have an orgasm.' They say to each other, 'Let's make love.' Love is a personal experience. So I begin this chapter with the description of a train of feelings that occur in sexual intercourse and that can be described psychologically. These feelings combine to give coitus a 'feel good' factor. They are not analysed by the couple as they are here. Intercourse, as with any repetitive behaviour, is carried out because of its intrinsic value. It does something for the couple which enhances their love for one another. This personal language is described in terms of affirmation of identity, affirmation of sexual identity, self-esteem, relief of distress, reconciliation and thanksgiving.

Affirmation of identity

Identity is a psychological concept that gives us the feeling of who we are in an ever-changing continuity from childhood to old age. It is the psychological passport to our existence. Work and relationship are the main contributors to identity. Normally we take our identity for granted. It is an unconscious presence. But from time to time we stop and reflect who we are, what we are doing and what our purpose in life is. This usually happens when there is a crisis, but may also occur when things are going well.

In this world of identity, sexual intercourse plays a vital part. Every time a couple who are in a continuous relationship (usually marriage, but not always so), make love, they are saying to each other, 'I recognise you. I want you. I need you. I appreciate you.' It is an exchange which says first of all that, of all the infinite possibilities of choice, the spouse has been recognised as the most important person in the world. When something happens to us, it is common to ask the question, 'Why me?' In sexual intercourse the body answers this question. Nobody else is being selected. Week after week, month after month, year after year, there is the acknowledgement that the spouse matters above all others. Although repetition may dilute the message, it is a message of supreme importance.

This explains the associated consternation surrounding jealousy and episodes of adultery. We become accustomed to being recognised above anyone else and to being chosen as such. Of course it is the relationship that makes the selection, but it is intercourse that gives it unique significance. This repetitive singular recognition extends its meaning to say that the choice is one of appreciation. Indeed, when the appreciation begins to falter or disappear, often intercourse does too. The spouse one makes love to may have faults, may be imperfect, may have caused pain or may have disappointed but, despite all his or her limitations, is appreciated for who he or she is. Intercourse is an act of faith in who the person is and what they hopefully may become.

At the beginning of marriage intercourse is an expression of the idealisation in which we hold our spouse. At the start he or she is felt to be perfect, and intercourse is an expression of that feeling. With the passage of time, flaws appear in the personality. These are recognised and idealisation is reduced. Nevertheless, a solid experience of the goodness of the partner remains and the measure of the recognition is translated into coitus. Intercourse is saying, 'You may not be perfect, but you are good enough.' This appreciation goes on through intercourse until death or until the relationship ends.

With the passage of time, the initial idealisation fades, but new depths of goodness and meaning are found. Intercourse verifies these new discoveries. It is the act that communicates and asserts the continuing discovery of each other. Finally, in this personal exchange, intercourse is saying that the spouses want each other. Every act of sexual intercourse is a renewal of the marriage vows. It is saying that, despite the passage of time, the couple need and want one another. Couples are aware of these feelings, and language is another way of expressing these meanings. Sexual intercourse is the visible and physical way of declaring these nuances and feelings. Altogether they add up to a powerful attestation of affirming one's identity. Just as our parents are the persons who gave us our identity in our childhood, so spouses continue to affirm each other in adulthood. God is the author of our identity. This identity is transmitted in an ambassadorial fashion by our parents when we are children and by our spouses when we are adults.

Sexual identity

We come to each other in life as sexual persons. Sociology defines gender in terms of the femininity and masculinity of the person. It takes into consideration the way we dress, talk, act, the things we do and the roles we assume. In sexual intercourse we summarise and express all these characteristics in and through our bodies. In receiving each other's bodies, we accept the talents we cherish in each other. Through intercourse, we make available the strengths and weaknesses of our masculinity and femininity and, genitally, we are saying to each other what sort of person we are in our gender.

Part of this gender manifestation is the whole exchange of action in intercourse. Who takes the initiative to suggest intercourse? In what way is the initiative made? Through a look? Touch? Word? This liturgy of exchange is a private code of sexual communication. It is part of the sexual signalling system between couples. They are speaking to each other through sexual desire and, as we have seen, it is a divine language. It is here also that there is an exchange of personal power between the couple. Who has the confidence and temerity to ask? Who has the confidence and temerity to suggest a particular sexual position? In this sexual exchange the couple are testing initiative, confidence and certainty, and are drawing out the fears of rejection, guilt and uncertainty. Beyond the drama of erotic invitation, there is the actual celebration of the body itself. The man makes the women feel fully sexual. In the course of ordinary life she is aware of her breasts, face, buttocks, thigh and belly, but now, as her partner takes pleasure in them, she delights in her sexuality. Her sexuality comes to life in and through her body, and thus she rejoices in her sexual identity. This is what the Song of Songs celebrates. The same occurs vice versa and the woman awakens the sexual identity of the man.

Sexual intercourse gives two verifications of the personality – the personal and the sexual – and, with the passage of time, sexual intercourse becomes a powerful source of giving to each other an awareness of who we and they are. In intercourse and through the two parameters, the individual changes from being an object of impersonal adoration and simple sexual desire or lust, to being a person of subjective awareness and love. The couple mutually endows each other with personal meaning. It takes decades to convert the initial idealisation to an enduring personal meaning and sexual intercourse plays a central part in this transformation.

Self-esteem

Modern psychology has made us aware that at the heart of our personality is the way we feel about ourselves. There is a world of difference between feeling and not feeling good about who we are and what we can do. It is no exaggeration that self-esteem gives courage, initiative, perseverance and achievement in our life. The alternative is doubt, uncertainty, fear, anxiety, self-deprecation and ultimately depression.

We gain our self-esteem from two sources: the feeling of being lovable and the worth of our achievement. Our parents gave us a mixture of acceptance and vindication of ourselves, and also our uncertainty. Psychoanalysis argues convincingly that our adult self-esteem has its roots in our childhood. Genetic contribution also plays a part, but our upbringing is crucial.

As already indicated, spouses take over where parents leave off. Spouses have two main levers with which to achieve their ends: first, in the quality of the relationship and secondly, in sexual intercourse. Sexual intercourse is a continuing thread in establishing the spouse's lovability and goodness. In the space of a few minutes spouses emerge from intercourse with a feeling of well-being. He or she feels really loved. This is one characteristic of sexual intercourse. The actual sexual exchange of the act itself is another. Did the couple really express fully the potential of their bodies? Did touch, penetration and sensation, conjoined with erotic feeling, convey fully the genital consummation? This is the world of sexual technique and, when things go wrong, of pathology.

Over time couples acquire the art of how to please one another. They know the right combination of positioning, touch, thrusting and massaging that gives full expression to sexual pleasure, the culmination of which tension asserts the goodness and self-esteem of each other. This self-esteem draws its strength from the relationship of the couple, culminating in intercourse that expresses physical erotic accomplishment and, in turn, personal affirmation.

Relief of distress

Couples enter their bedroom to make love, full of the realities of daily life. They may be tired, anxious, depressed, preoccupied, worried about their work or the children, their relatives and their personal traumas. Intercourse has a variety of relaxing experiences. It is par excellence a psychosomatic event in which the psyche influences the soma. There is the widespread myth of the wife, who does not want to have sex, complaining of a headache. There is very little description of the aftermath of intercourse as a soothing, relieving, relaxing experience in which physical and mental discomfort is relieved. Here the language of intercourse is medicinal. It is the relief of distress. This distress is both physical and psychological. Depression and anxiety are very common. The features of depression are mood change, tiredness, irritability, lack of concentration and of the feeling of well-being. Sometimes the depression is so severe that sexual intercourse is out of the question. But when present to a lesser degree, sexual intercourse can be a successful remedy. I well remember one of my patients, who was getting fed up with medication, declaring that the best remedy for depression was, as he put it, 'a good shag'.

Reconciliation

Intimacy in couples invariably leads to friction, conflict, quarrels and pain. This is an inevitable aspect of interpersonal closeness. Most of these conflicts are resolved, forgiven and forgotten quickly. But some are more severe and the pain is more persistent. The pain and withdrawal may last days, weeks or even longer periods. During this time the partners feel offended and hurt, and avoid each other. They may find apologies difficult or insufficient. It may take time for the pain to subside. Finally, it does subside and they make love. Sexual intercourse is now a language of forgiveness and reconciliation. It is the moment when they return to embrace each other as lovers. Hurt subsides. There is a real examination of conflict and, after intercourse, verbal communication may be restored and further healing takes place.

Thanksgiving

How do couples celebrate their mutuality? They may give presents to each other. They may take each other out for a meal. They may say verbally to each other, 'thank you'. Sexual intercourse can be the most powerful way of saying thank you to each other. Through intercourse, their complete availability to each other, they express thanks for being together yesterday, today and hopefully tomorrow. It is a recurrent act of their eucharistic experience.

The above six dimensions of personal encounter are actualised by sexual intercourse at any time in the course of marriage. But with the passage of time the couple find in intercourse a deeper personal meaning. These six meanings stand out but are not exhaustive. In the theology of *Humanae Vitae*, there is a unitive and procreative dimension. The above description enlarges that unitive meaning extensively.

Chapter 10

Sexual Intercourse and Interpersonal Love

The process of falling in love, however mysterious, is well documented and easily recognisable. But after a short time, months, perhaps years, the intensity of the experience fades, and yet marriage continues for several decades afterwards. What keeps the marriage going? How does love change?

In a series of books[1] and numerous articles I have investigated the process from falling in love to loving. I have suggested that there are three characteristics that encapsulate the main features of loving. These are sustaining, healing and growth. In nearly 20 years of enunciating this view, nobody has challenged it and, as far as I know, nobody has offered an alternative. This does not mean that there is not one, but it does mean that in these three parameters are contained the main interpersonal ingredients of what people understand as love. These components have been culled from the literature on marriage, from psychology and, above all, from personal experience in counselling. I do not claim that they are exclusive, but as I have lectured in scores of places the description has rung true to many people.

These characteristics are the daily and changing features of a marital relationship. They are in turn serviced by sexual intercourse and it is these three features that I will describe below. In my understanding of sexual intercourse as something intimately linked with love and as an expression of it, I have tried to show that couples make love when their daily experiences are felt as loving. They express with their bodies what they feel with their hearts.

Sustaining

By sustaining I have in mind five features, which are part and parcel of the daily routine of life, and which communicate love to the couple through different behaviour characteristics. These five are availability, communication, demonstration of affection, affirmation and resolution of conflict. These are not arbitrary choices. They express the continuation of love from childhood to adulthood. The whole theme of love in my understanding of it, in other words its methodology, is to set out the components of that love in childhood and to see how they continue in adult relationships.

Availability

The child survives on – indeed, when very young, is utterly dependent on – the availability of parents to sustain it first of all physically. In marriage, the couple sustain each other physically in health and illness, through nourishment and intimacy. Psychologically, the presence of the parents creates an anchor for the security of the child. In adult life the same applies. Spouses give each other a sense of security. This security is subtle. As we grow up, we develop autonomy and independence, and so the adult relationship is one of interdependence. Couples complement each other. When the couple are physically together, the company of each other, their presence, gives them a feeling of being recognised, wanted and appreciated. A walk, a meal and spending time together are ways in which they register each other through vision, sound, touch and smell. After being together for some time, their awareness of each other is enhanced and they want to consummate this reality through sexual intercourse. There are two things to be said about this. Firstly, that the presence of one another acts as a sexual trigger stimulus. Testosterone, which in the male is the source of the sexual drive, does not operate alone. It needs a fertile soil within which to grow. This fertile soil is the togetherness, but the togetherness is not any togetherness. It is a special one of an affective bond, and so for sexual intercourse to occur we need an affective togetherness, sexual arousal and a desire for completion of the presence of each other. Secondly, in our age, as often both husband and wife work, availability is at a premium. Not only that but when couples approach one another they are often tired. These are the obstacles to intimacy that present-day life offers. When these obstacles are overcome, coitus takes place that in turn reinforces the bonding.

Absence is destructive of the quality of intimacy. We experience longing for each other when we are apart. When couples have been away from each other, often the first thing they want to do when they return is to make love. Whether they are apart or together, sexual intercourse seals the physical awareness of the other.

Communication

Physical presence and the body define the most basic characteristic of existence and love. The young child experiences life through touch. Physical presence expresses one definition of existence, verbal communication another. It is through words that couples reveal to each other their inner world. They reveal who they are, what they think and feel, and what they think and feel about each other. In modern marriage communication has become a key expression of love. When the relationship deteriorates, so does communication.

Words reveal the inner world of each other and the consequent awareness seeks to find a concrete way to be understood. Sexual intercourse becomes that signal. Coitus after communication is a sign of understanding and accepting what has been said, and at the same time indicates that the spouses are ready to receive further disclosures about each other.

Communication is not always complete. It may be incomplete, confused, unsatisfactory or even critical. There comes a time when words fail to convey the message. That is where intercourse takes over. The subsequent enhancement of each other gives the confidence to explore further with words and to clarify matters. Words and coitus are in tandem with one another to bring interaction to a deeper level. The body affirms and also encourages further exploration. Sexual intercourse after verbal communication is a form of assent that the message has been received and, if not received, that the couple remain open for further communication.

The body affirms the word and through sex there is a total communication of the whole person.

Demonstration of affection

As a child, especially a young child, touch, kisses and caresses convey the affective dimension of love. Couples continue to demonstrate their affection for one another through looks, touch, kisses and caresses. This dimension is one of the clearest indicators of loving. There are two strands to demonstrating affection. The first is as a preliminary to sexual intercourse. The second is in the course of everyday life when the gestures are detached from sexual intercourse. In the course of my work as a marriage counsellor, I frequently hear the complaint, often from the wife, that her husband never tells her he loves her. The need to be reminded that one is loved with words and gestures is an essential part of loving and one that men particularly often neglect. Affectionate gestures before sexual intercourse and in the course of daily life are an essential feature of love.

Affirmation

Childhood is a time of development. One of the most powerful sources of this development is the affirmation the child receives from its parents, teachers and others. As with affection, this affirmation is needed in adult life. When we do something well we want to be appreciated. Spouses are ever present to acknowledge each other.

After appreciation a glow enters our being which wants celebration and the celebration is to be found in sexual intercourse. Couples, of course, celebrate with meals, presents and their sense of feeling good. Sexual intercourse is the most focused and frequent event which gives expression to this celebration of having said or done something well. Not only is sexual intercourse a sign of affirmation, but it is also a sign of encouragement and hope for the future.

Once again, in marriages that experience difficulties, affirmation is missing. There the couple keep their mouths shut when things go well and open them in order to criticise. Criticism can of course

be constructive, but it needs to be balanced either by an introduction or a completion of affirmation.

Resolution of conflict

One of the myths that people hold is that intimate relationships are
without conflict, but it is well established that the two are close
partners. Conflict is an inevitable part of intimacy and out of it
there stems personal growth. Conflict which is discussed shows the
partners what they want from each other, what the strife is about
and what is missing from the exchanges in the life of the couple.
This conflict is painful and, when it is resolved or as part of the
process of resolution, sexual intercourse occurs. Sexual intercourse
is part of the reconciliation process. Conflict is thought of as a
destructive sequence, but it is not and it is frequently present in the
lives of ordinary couples. Sexual intercourse and resolution of
conflict are very close and play a prominent part in their life.

In these five dimensions there is an interpersonal exchange
between loving and sexual intercourse. Of course these are not
exhaustive and can be added to, but they provide a prominent and
significant basis for loving.

Healing

Beyond sustaining, there is healing of which basically we have three
forms: physical, psychological and sexual. Physical healing is seen
in Western society, where few childhood diseases leave their impact
on adulthood. The second form of healing, psychological healing,
is needed because we emerge from childhood as wounded people.
These wounds are brought about by what goes wrong in the first
intimate experience of life. This intimate experience is the foundation of love in our life and so the wounds are those in the realm
of feeling loved.

In their interpersonal relationships, men and women are pre-
vented from registering, digesting and integrating love by lack of
self-esteem and confidence, insecurity, bouts of depression and
anxiety, rejection, guilt, uncertainty, fear and the accompanying
variety of phobias. When these conditions are severe, they need

expert attention. Interpersonal relationships are not only occasions when wounds emerge, but are also occasions for healing. Marriage is the most common second intimate relationship of love that gives an opportunity for healing.

How does this healing take place? The first model is psycho-dynamic. In the security of the marital relationship, the individual lets go of their defences created to protect the wound. As a result, the wound is exposed and the partner has a chance to provide a second opportunity to remove the wound or to offer the missing ingredient for healing, for example, acceptance, affirmation, appreciation, encouragement and so on. Of course, it takes time for healing to take place, which is why continuity of the relationship is essential. Another model of healing is the cognitive process. Here the individual slowly learns to give up the negative thoughts and behaviour that saturate their personality. The partner encourages the extinction of these negative thoughts and behaviour, and slowly positive thoughts and behaviour are built in their place. Between them these processes produce a transformation in the personality.

As men and women slowly change to become more accepting, secure and confident, feeling wanted and appreciated, so they participate in sexual intercourse as changed people. Coitus itself induces the change as the love transmitted through the body acts as a personal encouragement and affirmation.

Beyond physical and psychological healing, there is sexual healing. We have now come to realise how widespread sexual abuse is in childhood. As a result of traumatic sexual experiences, some adults reach their sexuality accompanied by fear, mistrust, disgust, anxiety and/or guilt. It is here that gentle, reassuring and loving sexual intercourse can give the person, usually the wife, the feeling that sex can be a welcome, good experience, surrounded by trust against mistrust, relaxation against tension and fear, the ability to enjoy the experience against feeling guilty and finally to feel sexual without feeling shame or distress.

We need to raise the profile of healing. We are accustomed to reading accounts of marital breakdown and the conflict surrounding divorce. We read nowhere about the result of healing which takes place in many marriages, indeed in millions of them. There is little doubt that a good marriage achieves more in healing than all the therapy that takes place in psychotherapy.

Growth

Finally, beyond sustaining and healing, we have growth. Over time a couple change and develop physically, socially and psychologically. Except for physical change, the other two occur imperceptibly and are not always visible to the couple. But their friends and relations, and those who see them frequently, can notice the difference. We grow in a variety of ways, as we shall see below.

There is a growing awareness of self. The most notable dimension is a shift from dependence to independence and then finally to interdependence. At the beginning of a marriage we may tend to rely on our partner to make decisions, take the initiative and tell us what to do. Little by little we find our confidence and assume more responsibility for ourselves. We grow into independence. We become more assertive. But there is a danger here for the relationship. We can become too independent and outgrow our partner. The key to a successful relationship is to become interdependent, to continue to need each other.

Beyond assertiveness we develop two characteristics. Slowly, sometimes very slowly, we become less egoistic. We grow much more aware of the other person. We get in touch with their feelings, their needs, their ways. We move from egoism to sharing and even to becoming lovingly altruistic and generous.

As our basic needs are met, so we can go beyond them to become aware of our spouse as a growing person, to appreciate what our partner needs and to give it to them. We become not only more altruistic but also more sensitive to each other, that is to say more empathetic. We are able to read the inner world of our partner more accurately. We assess their mood more clearly and respond to it more sensitively. Another feature of our growth is creativity. With the passage of time we develop skills, initiatives and ideas to create. The creation may be a new recipe, a do-it-yourself achievement, or a change of direction in our work or leisure activities. With this creativity there is also doubt. We are unsure whether we shall succeed and the reassurance and encouragement of our partner is vital. In the sexual field we give expression to all these changes by making love with a new awareness of ourselves. Although coitus may appear to be the same, we are now different people carrying it out.

We may also find the confidence to tell our partner about hidden erotic wishes, which hitherto we were afraid to communicate because of the fear of being rejected. We have more confidence to display our sexual feelings without diffidence. Not only do we carry out intercourse as different people, but we may also carry out intercourse itself with a deeper and wider meaning.

And so at the conclusion of these two chapters, we can see that sexual intercourse is more than an orgasm. The physical pleasure accompanying it both initiates, is accompanied by, and leads to personal appreciation and interpersonal loving communication. Sexual intercourse is not an isolated event. It is an essential component of the ongoing interaction of the couple. Physical pleasure is a language that alerts the couple to their personal meaning and love for each other. In this sense, while the isolated sexual act outside an ongoing relationship may have spectacular meaning for the two people involved, generally it is devoid of most of its possibilities. The isolated act of coitus is often deprived of its personal and interpersonal meaning and, despite its personal appearance, it is a beautiful car without an engine. Its potential lies in the meaning it gives to an ongoing relationship and, outside it, it is impoverished.

Moving on to the spiritual dimension, we have seen in the opening chapters of the book how intercourse in its sexual dimension was steeped in suspicion, hostility and fear. In due course it became reluctantly accepted through procreation and it remained in the context of this understanding until very recently. Then in the last 30 years all the Christian Churches have moved from this position to accepting coitus as an expression of love. But few have explored the link between human and divine love. I will attempt to do so here.

First of all, we have already mentioned the Song of Songs in which sexual attraction and the body communicate the divine plan for human loving intimacy. In this passage of Scripture, seriously ignored in 2,000 years of Christian sexuality, we find that the body with its erotic components has the divine assent to the messages it communicates.

So in the course of ordinary life, when we find ourselves in the grip of being sexually attracted, far from being apprehensive, anxious and experiencing disgust, we can be sure that we are in the midst of divine approval. We are meant to appreciate God with our bodies and our ordinary personal communication is embodied.

We accept God as a creator who gives identity to the world he created through his love. He hands over this creation to human beings, whose bodies become the principal instruments of perpetuating this love through marriage, in which the chief feature, as we have seen, is sexual intercourse.

At the centre of sexual intercourse is the naked encounter of a man and a woman. Nakedness has been viewed with an eye of suspicion in the Christian tradition, and yet nakedness highlights sexual attraction and pleasure. This nakedness in the midst of sexual intercourse continues the divine plan of creation. The couple has returned to a world of safety, relaxation, peak excitation and celebration of pleasure. The physical and the emotional slide imperceptibly into the spiritual. The couple recapture the initial state of innocence, now redeemed through grace, and thus they return to the state described in Genesis: 'This is why a man leaves his father and mother and joins himself to his wife, and they become one body. Now both of them were naked, the man and his wife, but they felt no shame in front of each other' (Gen. 2:24–25).

It is a common social phenomenon that when sexual matters are referred to in public a certain unease emerges which is translated into jokes or laughter. Similarly, the presentation of nakedness in public, although shown repeatedly in recent times, is still surrounded with apprehension and unease. Yet in sexual intercourse within marriage, nakedness assumes its original innocence and the communication of divine love. So at the very centre of intercourse there is a divine presence in nakedness.

From nakedness there is a move towards sexual intercourse and, as I have already described, the body is mobilised for actual intercourse that culminates in the intense exquisite pleasure of the orgasm. The whole procedure of intercourse is a divine liturgy of love. We go to church and experience God at the mass or at any other service. In marriage, the couple has their own domestic church and at the centre of this church is the enactment of sexual intercourse. Sexual intercourse as a divine liturgy gives the couple the means to experience and create love. It celebrates the personal, interpersonal and creative encounter of love described in the previous two chapters.

In this sense sexual intercourse with its components of nakedness and genital encounter is the epitome of embodiment and is the channel of the divine. The couple, in the process of making love, are expressing the central liturgy of the domestic church. They are the couple in prayer, and sexual intercourse is the central and recurrent act of prayer of the couple. More specifically, when we come to sexual intercourse, it reflects the inner world of the Trinity in that the Trinity expresses the relationship of love of persons. The Father loves the Son, and the fruit of this love is the Spirit and all three are essentially one but completely separate. We find in sexual intercourse an interpersonal union of love in which, at the moment of consummation, the spouses are one and yet at the same time they are separate persons. This total communion of separate persons who become one is one of the most powerful examples to illustrate the Trinity.

Thus God as love is expressed in the original state of the innocence of nakedness. The act of intercourse is like the Eucharist feast in which we take in each other's bodies. It culminates in the trinity formed by two people becoming a third, single being in one union. Since sexual intercourse has such a powerful spiritual connotation and is the experience of the overwhelming majority of married people, its understanding, safeguarding and appreciation is a major part of evangelisation. Marriage and sexual intercourse are the people of God in prayer. The ability of Christianity to see this vision is the spiritual answer to divorce and to the trivialisation of coitus.

Chapter 11

Sexual Intercourse and Procreation

In the previous two chapters no mention was made of procreation, and yet in the Christian tradition procreation has played the leading role in giving intercourse its meaning. As recently as the Second Vatican Council in the sixties, when sexual intercourse was seen as a love that uniquely expressed marital love, the Council stated: 'Hence, while not making the other purposes of matrimony of less account, the true practice of conjugal love, and the whole meaning of the family life which results from it, have this aim: that the couple be ready with stout hearts to cooperate with the love of the creator and the saviour, who through them will enlarge and enrich his own family day by day'.[1] Whilst the Council raised the vision of conjugal love to unprecedented levels, still the Fathers clung to the pre-eminence of procreation. However, the analysis of sexual intercourse given in the last two chapters gives a different interpretation to its meaning. How does this contradiction come about?

Historically, there is no doubt that Christianity was embarrassed by sexual attraction and pleasure, and turned to procreation to salvage intercourse from dereliction. In doing so, it was disregarding the experience of the couple for whom procreation was not the primary intention. It is true that previous ages lacked the psychological know-how to analyse coitus. What couples did know is that they were sexually attracted to each other and that their love was the catalyst to having sex. It is strange, and in fact a serious error on the part of Christianity, that, steeped as its roots are in love, it did not take the path of exploring intercourse in terms of love.

Instead, frightened by sexual pleasure, it took the course of neutral-ising it in terms of procreation, and for nearly 2,000 years it got away with it. Not that children are not important. They certainly are, and their continuation and presence form one of the greatest miracles of creation. However, they are not normally the main focus of sexual intercourse, except when the couple are actively seeking to become pregnant.

What are the factors that have shifted attention from procreation to love as the primary purpose of sexual intercourse? Firstly, psy-chology has given us tremendous insights in to the meaning of person and personal intimacy. Secondly, a hundred years of sexology have made us more familiar with the mysteries of sex. We are now no longer frightened of sexuality. Indeed, we are in danger of trivialising it. This book aims to describe the wonder of sexual intercourse and at the same time to understand it as a miracle of human love, expressing divine love. It is already clear, and it will be made even clearer in due course, that the full potential of sexual intercourse is to be found in an ongoing, enduring, committed and faithful relationship. While procreation is one of its glories, it is not its chief glory, which lies in the promotion of personal love. Thirdly, sexual physiology has now taught us that a woman's body, which is essential for fertilisation, is strictly economical with its capacity for the fertilisation of the ovum. In the monthly cycle, the ovum is shed and is capable of being fertilised for five days at the most. The design from nature shows very clearly that not every sexual act is open to life, and there is nothing from this design that says that it should be necessarily open to new life.

Fourthly, the size of the family has been greatly reduced. In addition marvellous advances have been made in the care of preg-nancy, premature infants and post-natal care. Now parents can choose to have a small family, consistent with the global needs of the world and especially the demands of the care and education of children. As a result, most sexual intercourse has become surplus to procreation requirements. Not many sexual acts are needed to have a family of two to three children, and yet couples continue having sexual intercourse into their fifties, sixties, seventies and even longer. It is absolutely clear that the personal is more important than the procreative in sexual intercourse.

Fifthly, the arrival of safe and widespread contraception, which even the majority of Roman Catholics have embraced, allows the timing of procreation with precision and also the enjoyment of sexual intercourse when it is no longer needed for procreation. It has been part of the defence of the regulation of birth by natural means, that it is good for the couple to abstain from intercourse as a sign of chastity and self-control. This point of view has no insight into the personal meaning of coitus and sees it primarily as a pleasurable indulgence whose control is good for the person. This is not to say that control is not needed in sexual intercourse for a variety of reasons, such as ill-health and inappropriateness on other occasions, but it does mean that if we appreciate the personal meaning of sexual intercourse, then, if the couple desire it, procreation should not be a factor to prevent it.

It is still heard and written today that, if procreation is taken out of the centrality of sexual intercourse, then there is no moral basis for keeping the latter within marriage and casual sex will simply multiply. In fact, whilst casual sex has increased somewhat, the overwhelming majority of sex in Western society is not casual but takes place within committed relationships. We see too that, if procreation is no longer the main reason for confining intercourse to marriage, then what the integrity of the act requires is a relationship of continuity, commitment, exclusiveness and faithfulness in order to do justice to its personal and interpersonal meaning.

All this does not mean that procreation is not important. It does mean that we have to shift the emphasis from the biology of procreation, from what the Church has been obsessed with, namely the deposit of semen into the vagina, to the marvel of life itself. Intercourse is sacred because it mobilises life.

In the now obsolete language of the purposes of marriage before the Second Vatican Council, the primary purpose was the procreation and education of children. We have seen that society has diminished the importance of biological procreation in a world of food shortages and child poverty. The important factor now is education. The Catholic Church and indeed all Christian Churches have a good record in cognitive education. But for a religion steeped in love that considers that the essence of God is love, then education for being a loving person should be predominant.

What lies in the future is a kind of parenting in which the emotional wounds inflicted on children will diminish. I see the Church transferring its focus from procreation to an education for personal love. This subject requires a whole book in itself, but it is clear that parents have an immense responsibility to go beyond teaching children how to read and write and how to distinguish between right and wrong. Whilst we must still educate for the moral person, it is even more important to strive for the promotion of the loving person. As Christians we must explore the Scriptures to find what they teach us about love. If the main purpose of procreation is to educate the child to become a loving person, then what is the role of intercourse in procreation?

We have seen that the biology of procreation is a bygone priority. Sexual intercourse as a personal and nurturing experience of the couple is the key to sustain them in the labour of bringing up their children as loving persons. It is only now that we appreciate the time and responsibility that are needed to educate children to become loving persons. Patience, tolerance, tact, firmness, affirmation and time are all essential requirements. Parents do not always have them, or have them in the sufficient quantity that children need. One of the essential sources of this strength is the encouragement to be found in sexual intercourse. Those who are sceptical of the point of view expressed in this book, and particularly in the demise of the prominence of procreation, will point out that if procreation is not emphasised, then there will be a decline in births and women will not want to have and look after children. Fathers will become even more irresponsible and will not accept their responsibilities to support their partners and their children. There is no doubt that some women are not enthusiastic about having children. Some are not born nurturers and therefore desist from procreation. The answer to these problems is not to bully them to have children. If a small proportion of women do not procreate, the world will not come to an end. The important thing is to match procreation with the desire to nurture. Most women want to have children and we see this in the pain of the infertile. If quantity gives way to quality, then human beings will become more civilised and loving. Critics will say that fewer children are the mark of a selfish and hedonistic society. However, if numbers are replaced by love – and this must be the aim of Christianity – we have nothing to fear. There is no danger that procreation will cease and that sexual intercourse will become a centre for hedonism. Those who fear this do not see what riches sexual intercourse offers apart from pleasure. So I conclude this chapter with an understanding of sexual intercourse as being designed so that each act will promote life, and on some occasions new life.

Indeed, I would say further that all the characteristics outlined in the previous three chapters are neither ideal nor moral imperatives of sexual intercourse, but basic potentials which may be realised fully or partially.

Chapter 12

Sexual Difficulties

This book is not intended to be a manual of normal and abnormal sexual intercourse. There are plenty of those around. But some reading this book will consider that, so far, an idealised version of coitus has been presented. To put matters in perspective, this brief chapter shows some of the imperfections of sexual intercourse.

There are three main areas of difficulty with sexual intercourse. Firstly, there are the ordinary afflictions of tiredness, alienation and hostility. Secondly, there is a deterioration of the actual relationship itself, leading finally to divorce. Thirdly, there are a whole host of psychological difficulties that affect the sexual act itself. Let us consider briefly these three areas. Firstly, there is the daily toll of sexual casualties through tiredness. Most sexual intercourse takes place in the bedroom at night. Not infrequently couples come to bed tired and preoccupied. The only thing they want to do is go to sleep. Here there is often a different programme of needs. The man may want to have sex, but the wife often only wants a cuddle. If only men could appreciate the value of a cuddle, quite a lot of misunderstandings might never occur. Instead of being tired, the couple may come to bed preoccupied. They want to talk to one another. Once again, it may be the wife who wants to talk and the husband who wants to go to sleep. But talking, communication, is a valuable source of mutual love and, although the couple may stay awake until the early hours of the morning, much may be achieved.

Couples not only bring their preoccupations to bed, they also carry their feelings. So they may come to bed angry or hostile with each other. Again, it may be difficult for the man to understand. For him, sex can be, and often is, a mere physical reality. For the woman, it is surrounded with feelings and her disposition to make love often depends on how she feels. So what has gone on in the preceding 24 hours influences her mood for sex a great deal. She may be preoccupied with the children, with relatives, the home or work, or she may not feel well.

There are some aspects of a woman's life that particularly affect sexual intercourse. The time of the month may be important as some women get premenstrual tension and do not want to have sex. There is menstruation itself. For some, it is a taboo time for sex; for others, the physical barriers have been overcome.

Then there is the period after the birth of a child. For a lot of women their sexual drive diminishes after the birth and it may take months or even a year for normal desire to return. Some women, a good 10 %, suffer post-natal depression during which time they are not interested in sex. I recorded in my second book[1] a problem of persistent loss of sexual desire after the birth of a child. It had continued for about nine years and played havoc with the marital relationship.

A deteriorating marriage relationship is the second major reason for unsatisfactory sex. If ever any proof is needed that sex is linked with love, all we have to witness is the decimation of sexual intercourse as the marriage plunges into difficulties. This is not the place to describe the range of marital difficulties as I have done this elsewhere.[2] Basically, the couple may find that there is massive incompatibility after the initial idealisation has evaporated. These breakdowns occur early in the marriage. Later one partner may outgrow the other, and this is described as falling out of love.

Thirdly, there may be the introduction of severe alcohol, aggression, gambling or drugs. Fourthly, there may be a gradual disenchantment with each other. Whatever the reason, one of the earliest demonstrations of marital difficulties is the abatement of sexual intercourse. The link between sexual intercourse and love in the relationship is shown by the fact that sexual therapy, without improvement of the relationship, is of no avail.

Finally, reference to sexual therapy brings us into the world of the biology and physiology of sex. We understand a great deal more about both of these, and an invaluable textbook on the subject for those who are concerned is Bancroft's *Human Sexuality and its*

Problems.[3] This splendid book describes the anatomical, physiological and pathological aspects of sexuality.

Briefly, there is both in the male and the female the possibility of a fundamental problem of lack of sexual drive. Sexual desire fluctuates in both men and women, but what I am referring to here is its complete loss. There are both psychological and physiological reasons for this and, when present, expert advice is necessary.

In the man, the following problems are common. The first is premature ejaculation, which is the condition of an early orgasm and ejaculation of the sperm before the wife has had the chance to become excited and reach her own orgasm. The second common problem is impotence which, in the first half of life, is commonly due to psychological reasons and in the second half of life is due to physical ones. One of the many reasons for this is the failure of the vessels to dilate with blood and the widely-discussed Viagra has helped a lot of men with this.

In women there is the presence of vaginismus – persistent pain when having sexual intercourse. Also, women do not always have an orgasm from sexual intercourse and there are some who never experience it. Some women have been sexually abused in childhood and have difficulty in having sexual intercourse. Clearly the remedy for these ordinary, relationship and physical problems are various. Between them, they affect sufficient numbers to leave a gap between an idealised presentation of sexuality and reality. Thus it is not surprising that, when people compile a list of the important factors for marital happiness, sexuality does not often come to the top. Companionship is considered more important.

The point I am making is not that we should ignore sexual difficulties, but that we should assert that sexual intercourse has a rich potential to initiate and foster relationships. Although the relationship itself is important, sexual intercourse has hidden possibilities which have yet to be explored. Coitus is much more than a transient moment of pleasure and, although couples adapt to its absence, this is very often a rationalisation and they would much prefer to continue to make love.

The mushrooming and growth of sexual therapists and the flooding of people to them is an indication of how much sex is appreciated. Part of the historic acceptance of a limited sexual life is due to the Christian devaluation of its significance. On the other hand, the pornographic trivialisation of sex has not convinced people that titillation, which is all that it conveys, is a substitute for the rewards of a sexual life filled with integrity. This integrity is the result of hard work, and Christianity has a responsibility to raise the profile of making love. However, it is clear from the psycho-somatic link of sexual love that there will be occasions, especially for the woman, when the personal meaning of sexual intercourse described in this book will not necessarily be present or will be present in an attenuated form.

Chapter 13

Moral Implications
of Sexual Intercourse

In the traditional understanding of sexual intercourse as being inti-mately linked with procreation, the morality of sex was focused on having sexual intercourse in such a way that semen was discharged into the vagina. Consequently oral and anal intercourse were wrong. Masturbation was also wrong, because the seed was not deposited in the vagina. Intercourse was only valid within marriage, which provided for the care and education of the procreated child. Thus the morality of sexual intercourse was largely based on the natural law of the biology of the act and of procreation. This morality was the main springboard for looking at sexual sins for hundreds of years. In the absence of an understanding of the personal and interpersonal world of sexual intercourse in terms of love, crude biology prevailed. Clearly an understanding of the link between sex and love, as outlined in the Second Vatican Council and in Christian Churches in general, shifts the moral emphasis from biology to the quality of the relationship. What we are concerned with now are the characteristics that safeguard the expression of sexual inter-course as a personal act of love. What needs to be primarily preserved is not biology but the psychology of relationship.

Our first understanding of the psychology of relationship is in childhood. There the young child needs to be protected and nur-tured for a period of nearly two decades. The baby is helpless and needs feeding, cleaning, warmth, delicate handling, accurate response to its needs and gentleness. The childhood interpersonal relationship between parents and children requires commitment.

Commitment to another person is learnt in the care of children. There parents must remain continuously present, ever ready to respond, aware of the child at the expense of themselves, constant in the presence of fluctuating moods and continuously focused on the child. Commitment is also the first criteria of the inner world of sexual intercourse. There commitment is a characteristic of love of the relationship. Successful sexual intercourse needs the committed devotion of two people. This devotion means that, in the course of sexual intercourse, love is shown in the process of preparing the spouse for lovemaking. Men in particular can be hasty lovers whose only interest is to enter the woman and reach orgasm. This is not how women perceive sexual intercourse. Attention to feelings is vital. On the other hand, women may need to appreciate the physical urgency of their spouse. As already mentioned, for men sexual arousal is a process that is situated in time, while the atmosphere between the couple exerts a great deal of influence on the readiness of the wife to make love. This sets the background, the atmosphere, that precedes lovemaking. Then there is the actual preparation for successful intercourse. Lovemaking implies the mutual sexual arousal of the partners. A man needs to arouse his wife by touches, caresses and massaging the erotic parts of her body. Only when she is excited, does he enter her. It requires devotion and commitment to accomplish this.

In the future the morality of sexual intercourse will include how patient the spouses are to prepare each other for lovemaking and how patient and disciplined they are to reach orgasm together, thus ensuring that one does not peak earlier than the other, leaving one partner unsatisfied.

Commitment extends beyond personal care of the relationship, and is also devoted to the mutual satisfaction of pleasuring each other. Christianity has to learn that pleasure is not dangerous but is to be enjoyed and appreciated as a channel for communicating personal meaning. Thus commitment is a human characteristic that endows the relationship with permanency and, within that permanency, generates a concern to pleasure each other to the full.

Commitment is one overall characteristic that safeguards sexual intercourse. Another is that it must be placed within an enduring relationship. Continuity is a vital characteristic for successful sexual intercourse. Couples come to each other with their instinctual readiness to have sex. They know the biology of the act but, as we have seen, the crude outline of sex is modified and enriched by the gradual learning of the positions preferred, the form of excitation desired and the empathetic understanding of what pleasures each other. Thus the physical becomes a language for the pleasure of the personal. An enduring relationship allows the couples to explore their sexuality through different positions, methods of arousing each other, learning to reach a climax together and so on. It takes time to learn what pleasures each other. In this way every act of sexual intercourse can be a fresh revelation to each other.

An enduring relationship not only extends the mutual skills of lovemaking, but also allows the couple to learn more about each other and so place their lovemaking within the context of an ever-deepening understanding of each other. Sexual intercourse may appear to be the same each time, but this is not true. It is happening within a framework of an ever-changing mood for the act and also within the context of an ever-altering personality of the couple.

Couples who do not enjoy sexual intercourse tend to say that the act becomes habitual and loses its freshness. Against such feelings, the desire for a new sexual experience becomes actualised and this is the background for adultery.

It is important in an enduring relationship to pay attention both to the act and to physical appearance. In the new moral context of coitus, it is vital for the man and the woman to take care of their bodies and remain attractive.

Sexual intercourse has been found to be good for the health of the couple and an enduring relationship preserves the continuation of this health factor.

Beyond commitment and an enduring continuity, sexual intercourse needs exclusiveness. The prostitute is par excellence the person who forfeits exclusiveness. For him or her, sex is a public experience. Why does sexual intercourse need exclusiveness? There is something private in having sex with another person. We expose our nakedness, our helplessness, our vulnerability and we do not find this easy. Despite the apparent widespread presence of sexual intercourse, even in our day and time most of it takes place in committed, enduring and exclusive relationships. Sexual intercourse renders us helpless, helpless physically and emotionally. There is nothing more personal to offer to a partner. It is a situation that needs the maximum of safety. We want to be sure that we are not going to be attacked physically or emotionally. This means making love with someone we feel safe with, someone whose commitment we have tested and who has a continuing meaning for us. It means that our partner becomes an exclusive person to whom we can entrust our nakedness, our bodies, our vulnerability, our ecstasy. Sexual intercourse is such a delicate, mysterious act that it needs the maximum safeguard from threat and attack to make it feel safe.

We return time and again to the same person to whom, in our sexuality, we reveal the whole of ourselves. The body becomes the message for the whole of our selves. But there is another factor which exclusiveness contains. Mention has been made that falling in love is an experience that combines sexual attraction and personal compatibility in the setting of an affective bond or attachment. This attachment is based on an exclusive encounter through vision, touch, sound and smell. The exclusivity of the attachment lays down parameters within which we are not only physically safe but within which affectivity can function. To return to the prostitute, she can have sex with many people because she has no affective attachment to any of her clients. An affective attachment narrows down the persons we can make love to. In fact for most of us it narrows it down to one person. It is only when this bond or attachment becomes ambiguous, diluted or comes to an end that the person can shift their commitment to someone else. Adultery leaves a person in a confused state, feeling attached to one person and yet having intercourse with another. But adultery is often associated with guilt, and the guilt is the fruit of knowing that one belongs elsewhere. Sexual intercourse needs exclusivity for reasons of safety, physical and emotional, and for complying with the attachment to one and only one other person with whom we have formed an affectionate bond.

To commitment, permanency and exclusivity, we must add finally faithfulness. There are two reasons why faithfulness must surround sexual intercourse. Firstly, the man must know that the child he is supporting is his and, in the days when lineage was important, that his children would inherit the property and states belonging to the father. Secondly, sexual intercourse is a means through which the physical expresses the personal. A man or a woman feels recognised, wanted and appreciated through sexual intercourse. When their partner has coitus with somebody else, there is a personal threat to their significance. Their trust feels let down and they feel unwanted and rejected. Faithfulness is a means of showing the personal meaning of acceptance of another person. It is the most regular means of showing the exclusive significance of the other. From the time of birth we are born to an exclusive and faithful relationship with our parents, which continues with our spouses and which is designated through sexual intercourse.

We have now seen that, instead of sexual intercourse primarily safeguarding procreation, it is the quality of relationship that guards the characteristics of love and sexual intercourse. The principles of morality for sexual intercourse are those that safeguard its relational integrity. It is for this reason that in my book *Sexual Integrity*,[1] I use the word integrity as a better term to convey sexual morality than chastity. Chastity still conveys an atmosphere of protecting an act that is specifically dangerous. Integrity suggests that sexual intercourse has its own physical and emotional existence that needs safeguarding to do justice to its complex meaning.

So far I have described the physical, personal, interpersonal and spiritual meanings of intercourse and have suggested that to safeguard its integrity sexual intercourse needs to take place in an environment of a committed, enduring, permanent, exclusive and faithful relationship which is marriage. We have to distinguish between marriage, which has been understood as commonly agreed for a long time,[2] and the time when it begins, which has been in much dispute. What I am saying in this chapter is that the needs of the integrity of sexual intercourse coincide with what we have understood traditionally by marriage. It is not a long step for Christianity to move from understanding marriage as a place of procreation and the nurturing of children, to a relationship where the integrity of sexual intercourse is safeguarded.

In fact, we can come to the conclusion that marriage safeguards both the child and sexual intercourse, but the principal reason for coitus is personal and interpersonal love. Morality is to surround the act with the appropriate human behaviour to realise its potential.

Christianity has taken its meaning of marriage from St Augustine who postulated its three characteristics as *proles, fides* and *sacramentum*. At the time of St Augustine sexual intercourse was not appreciated for its human and divine potential. Now we know better, and what has been suggested is that part of St Augustine's definition applies equally well for the meaning of marriage as safeguarding the integrity of sexual intercourse. The moral implications of what I have written is that sexual intercourse is not only moral when procreation takes place, but is also moral whenever its integrity is safeguarded by a relationship of commitment, continuity, permanency, exclusivity and faithfulness. Furthermore, we shall have to pay increasing attention to a morality of the care and attention paid to making coitus successful and realising its physical, emotional and spiritual potential.

Part III

Burning Issues

Chapter 14

Teenage Sexual Intercourse

The Scriptures and Christian teaching are clear that sexual intercourse before marriage is fornication and is wrong. Our age has
seen a rise in premarital sexual intercourse. In my writings I have
specifically stated that all premarital sexual intercourse cannot be
judged in the same way as marital sexual intercourse. It makes a lot
of difference whether sexual intercourse takes place casually, in the
setting of cohabitation or adultery, or the night before the wedding.
In this and the next two chapters I shall examine premarital sexual
intercourse in various settings.

Wellings et al[1] documented that sexual intercourse is taking place
at an increasingly earlier age. Amongst women aged 55–59 at the
time of interview, born between 1931 and 1935, the median age at
first sexual intercourse was 21 years. For those born between 1936
and 1940, it falls to 20, and further still to 19 for those born between
1941 and 1945. The median age for the youngest first cohort, those
aged 16–24 and born between 1966 and 1975, was 17 years old. The
recent study of the Social Exclusion Unit on teenage pregnancy[2]
shows that the number of young people sexually active by the age
of 16 doubled between 1965 and 1991, with the rise most striking
for girls. It is estimated that nearly 27 % of boys and 18 % of girls
are sexually active by the age of 16.

Some of the fall in the age at first intercourse reflects the falling
ages of sexual maturity, thanks to the improvement in general health
and diet. Why do young people start having sex? Firstly, there is no
doubt that as a result of the sexual revolution, society and the media
bombard the young with erotic and romantic stimulation. Secondly,
there is a general drop in importance of religious prohibition.

Thirdly, the link between sex and procreation has all but disappeared, and with it the main platform of Christian teaching for 2,000 years has gone. The failure of Christianity to produce a credible alternative morality for sex to the link between procreation and sexual intercourse is serious and one of the biggest defects of Christian moral teaching. Retreating to the past, to fundamentalism or to obsolete teaching is no answer. Research by the Social Exclusion Unit has discovered that the reasons for starting sexual intercourse include curiosity, popularity, real or imagined peer pressure, the desire not to be left behind, being in a relationship, fear of losing boy or girlfriend, the need to feel loved and the belief that sex equals love, and media influences that glamorise sex, alcohol and drugs.

In the absence of an adequate education, young people, particularly boys, feel pressure in their bodies to have sex. Here Christianity is particularly responsible for its inadequate sexual education, but society as a whole is also at fault. The last 50 years have seen widespread biological sexual education, but no teaching on feelings and emotions that are the key to understanding sexual intercourse. There are two responses to sexual curiosity. One is to experiment; the other is to appreciate the richness, mystery and sacredness of sexual intercourse and to wait until this is realisable. The world has trivialised sex. The Churches have been slow, afraid, confused and hesitant to explore this rich divine gift. The result is a vacuum that the young fill as best they can.

After curiosity comes having the opportunity for sex. This is rampant. What with parties, school and the use of the motor car, there is no shortage of opportunity.

Real or imagined peer pressure is a very real entity. Adolescents are rebelling from parents and pursuing their autonomy. They want to be considered adult, mature and experienced. Smoking, drugs, alcohol and sex have become the symbols of adulthood. The answer to this is a right relationship between the teenager and parents which allows autonomy, and yet is one in which the parents retain respect and are listened to. By and large, the Churches have lost their authority in all fields and particularly in the specific area of sexuality. Parents, teachers and youth leaders are left without guidance, and a much more penetrating and authentic understanding of sexuality is needed before these groups will be listened to. The desire not to be left behind is again very real. The teenager and the adolescent are people in a hurry. They want to become adults in double quick time. Sexual intercourse is what adults do. Losing one's virginity is a sign of adulthood. What is needed is an education to show that what adults try to do is to love one another. Sex is part of the process of loving one another. Young people need to link adulthood with love and not necessarily with sex. The instincts with which they are endowed do not make them persons. Reason and love do, and an education that does not prepare for feelings is dismally inadequate.

Some young people try sex because they think they are in a loving relationship. Their minds are filled with romantic thoughts. Falling in love is one of the most frequent reasons for having sex. 'I love him/her' is the commonest excuse. There is no doubt that love is the most complicated human experience. So far in this book I have made it clear that our first love experience is in childhood in the hands of our parents. The care we receive there is our tutorship for being recognised, wanted and appreciated. According to John Bowlby's model (see Chapter 6), we form an emotional, affective attachment through vision, sound, touch and smell. Young people fall in love with one another in this way. Falling in love is a complex of sexual attraction and affective attachment, but that is also the basis of infatuation. We cannot easily distinguish between infatuation and falling in love, and young people often have sex when they are merely infatuated.

Genuine loves needs, in addition to sexual attraction and affective attachment, emotional and social compatibility. We need to know whether we are really suited to each other before we can confirm that we are really in love. There is no easy way to test between genuine love and infatuation. For young people reading this passage the crucial test is whether you would want to be with this person for the rest of your life. The trouble with affective attachment, which is the most common basis for thinking that one is in a loving relationship, is that you can fall out of a loving attachment just as easily as you fell into it.

Traditionally, we have taught young people, indeed all people, to discipline their instincts and to have control over their feelings.

Young people feel their instincts are something good and do not see why they should deny themselves. The answer is not in the word denial. To deny something good makes no sense. To set something good in its proper relationship, because only then does it feel fully worthwhile, makes a lot of sense. What we have to teach young people are the characteristics of genuine love which are sexual attraction, emotional attachment and personal compatibility which has been found to be enduring. This takes time. Relationship is a time to find out whether they exist. Sexual intercourse should not be the basis for exploring whether a loving relationship exists. Sexual intercourse is the fulfilling symbol of a loving relationship.

The boy or girl who is threatened that their friend will leave if they don't have sex is clearly under pressure and emotional duress. The fear of being alone, of never finding another friend, or of being rejected are real psychological entities. Clearly loving is more than exerting pressure. The pressure often put on the girl by the boy is not love but the manifestation of the male hormone testosterone.

Self-esteem is the key to the necessary resistance. Traditional Christian teaching emphasised the power of the will to resist temptation. We know now that self-esteem is the key to resist temptation. Self-esteem gives the young man or woman the robustness to cope with rejection and/or temporary aloneness with the conviction that if they feel and are lovable, then someone else will come to replace those coercing them.

The need to feel loved and the belief that sex equals love is of great significance. The adolescent is in a period of transition. He/she is growing away from the parents and feels alone and at times abandoned. They desperately need to be loved. But love does not necessarily equal sex. Sex is the manifestation and confirmation of an existing loving relationship. What the adolescent needs are strong bonds and friendship. Friendship is an experience that both society and Christianity have greatly undervalued, and is very important for support.

Everybody needs to feel loved, including the adolescent and especially the deprived adolescent. It has been well documented that boys and girls who have had an emotionally deprived childhood either through poor parenting, being brought up in an institution or through marital breakdown, are particularly hungry for affection and are more ready to have sexual intercourse early. Those who are deprived emotionally are particularly prone to becoming pregnant. A baby gives them the feeling of being wanted and needed. They have something they can call their own, something which they can look after.

The influence of the media is also undoubtedly very great. It glamorises sex and we are bombarded by sexual messages. These messages in fact trivialise sex because they portray sexual attraction without the elaboration of affective attachment and personal compatibility. Nor do they give a clue to the inner world of sex as portrayed in this book. The bombardment of sex from the media will continue in the immediate future. What is needed is a strong religious and educational counter influence.

Finally, we have the youth culture of alcohol and drugs. There is no doubt that alcohol reduces inhibitions and allows sexual intercourse to take place in the most unpromising circumstances. Control of alcohol is something that parents and other supervisors can exert and in this way can help safeguard their teenage children. The same can be said about drugs.

It is the specific aim of this book to show that the link between sex and procreation, important as it is, is no longer the prominent thrust and reason for sexual intercourse. The main reason for having sex is the initiation and facilitation of love. Christianity has to get this message clear. The prohibition of fornication is not enough. Language is very important and fornication has no longer the prohibitive tone that it had in previous generations. But that does not mean that its meaning is obsolete. As in so many other areas, Christianity has to unpack its language. With reference to teenage sex, why is it wrong for adolescents to have sexual intercourse? The answer 'Because the Church says so' has very little influence. Young people have to appreciate the meaning of sexual intercourse. Sexual intercourse is there to seal a loving relationship, which is more than falling in love. As has been repeatedly asserted, love involves the presence of sexual attraction, emotional attachment and personality compatibility. Adolescents and teenagers certainly have the biological and physical capacity to have sex. But biology does not equip us to provide love in a relationship. This is why the isolated one-night stand bears no relationship to the presence of love. Beyond biology, we need a loving bond or attachment. This gets us nearer to what we understand by being in love but, as I have shown, sexual attraction and sexual attachment are not enough. Sexual attachment may be present, but we may fall out of love with the same person.

We need the third element in place that is a harmony, compatibility and suitability of the personality and that takes time to discover. Sex as a hasty, casual, promiscuous event is incompatible with love.

One final matter before this chapter is closed. It is a strong belief in conservative circles that contraception has facilitated early and easy sex. The document *Teenage Pregnancy* from the Social Exclusion Unit states that between a third and a half of sexually active teenagers do not use contraception at first intercourse. The point behind this startling figure which is not appreciated is that a great deal of sexual activity is prompted by impulsive, instinctual behaviour which is not easily open to rational processes. The key to reducing unloving or immature sex is not the banning of contraception. This belief is a myth, tenaciously clung to by those who are unable to move forward in understanding sexuality in terms of love. In any case, if youngsters are going to have sex, contraception helps to avoid pregnancy and the transmission of disease.

Changes in social habits can only be achieved through the education of the meaning of human behaviour. The link between procreation and sex persisted for 2,000 years because it made sense of human behaviour. It no longer makes sense and we have an obligation to young people to make sense of sex in terms of person, relationship and love. We have to show them that losing one's virginity is not a sign of maturity. It is not a hurdle to be negotiated. We have to show that coitus is the beginning of a journey of personal love, which is the key to interpersonal survival and is a mystery. There are no quick solutions such as prohibiting contraception. The Church needs first of all to understand interpersonal love in terms described in this book and further elaborated by others. It must convey this message ceaselessly, and parents and teachers must unpack the message. The body is the site of the holy. Holiness is love in relationship, and that is the Trinity.

Chapter 15

Cohabitation

In the previous chapter we saw that for a variety of reasons young-sters try sex which is immature, in the sense that their bodies are ready for intercourse but their emotions are not mature enough to realise the inner potential of its meaning. After the age of 16, sexual activity increases. In previous generations all sex, considered as fornication, was prohibited before marriage. Gareth Moore writes, 'Since sex was ordained by God for the purpose of bringing children into the world, the proper context for it was within marriage, since children need a loving and stable environment; this was provided by marriage, which was for the raising of children and has so been instituted by God himself. From this it followed that premarital sex or adultery was forbidden.'[1] From this it also followed that all sexual activity that was not orientated to procreation was forbidden. Moore states that this view was often more honoured in the breach than in the observance, and that a great deal of this forbidden sexual activity went on among Christians, including the official spokesmen.

The traditional view, which forbad both masturbation and sex before marriage, was obeyed by few and disobeyed by many, but the official teaching of the Church was not challenged. The belief that sex should be postponed until after marriage was the fruit of centuries of a Christianity that devalued sexuality, was suspicious of sexual pleasure, had a mystical belief in the power of the will and self-control, and propagated a view of sexual morality that held together in theory at least. It no longer holds together and one of the greatest demonstrations of its demise is the widespread presence of cohabitation. This chapter examines the implications of cohabitation: firstly the incidence, secondly the reasons and thirdly the moral implications.

Among first unions which started in the 1950s and the first half of the 1960s, virtually all were marriages which were not preceded by premarital cohabitation. By the early 1980s, about one half of first unions were marriages without prior cohabitation. Put another way, by the late 1980s about 40 % of first unions were marriages without premarital cohabitation, while a further 40 % were marriages with premarital cohabitation and around 20% were cohabiting unions.[2] These figures are for Britain, but in the same issue figures from Western society were given and suggest that in most west and north European countries cohabitation has eclipsed marriage as the marker for the first partnership, whereas in southern Europe it continues to be marriage. In many west and north European countries, with Britain being one of the exceptions, there is little evidence that the propensity to become a couple has declined, as cohabitation has simply replaced some of the marriages of yesteryear. In most countries cohabiting unions still tend to be short-lived, either converting to marriage or dissolving.

Clearly this development of cohabitation has occurred in the last 40 years in the aftermath of the sexual revolution of the twentieth century. Young people do not accept the traditional view that the period between puberty and marriage should be without sex. This is something that Christianity has to face.

Another reason for cohabitation in these four decades is that young people who engage in it are often the sons and daughters of broken marriages. They have seen the pain and chaos of divorce and they want to test their relationship before they proceed to marriage. There is evidence across all nations that children who experience parental divorce are more prone to cohabitation.

Further, society has become more secular. Adherence to religious mores has receded and couples do not feel uncomfortable in cohabiting. There is evidence in all Western societies that cohabiting couples come from the more secular section of society.

Why do couples convert cohabitation into marriage? Cohabitation is a short-lived affair, under two years on average. When couples who have moved from cohabitation to marriage gave their reasons for this step, 34 % replied that they wanted to strengthen the relationship or make it more secure, 21 % that the step was connected with having children and 8 % that the trial had worked. It is clear from these figures that for many people cohabitation is a prelude to marriage and that coupling in a non-promiscuous way is the established order in contemporary society. But, even given these reassuring statistics, what is the moral status of cohabitation? One view, which is the orthodox Christian position, is that marriage occurs in a wedding in church and anything else is fornication. The other view is that cohabitation is a marriage in its own right. Let us examine the latter position.

One of the earliest and most persistent understandings of marriage in Christianity was and still is that the essentials of marriage are free consent, meaning commitment, and sexual intercourse, meaning consummation. This was the position of the Roman Catholic Church prior to 1564 and of the Anglican Church in England and Wales prior to 1754, when a ceremony in church before a priest and two witnesses became essential. As far as the Roman Catholic Church was concerned, this legislation after the Council of Trent was social in origin. Clandestine marriages, in which men in particular pledged themselves to several women at the same time, made it hard for the marriage tribunals to decide who was the legitimate wife of any particular husband. Hence the legislation, but this did not add anything to the essentials of when a marriage is a marriage.

There is thus a case to be made for cohabitation in so far as it is an exclusive, committed, enduring and faithful relationship, consummated by sexual intercourse, to be considered as marriage. It does not fit in with the idea of a marriage service in church but it fits in perfectly with the essentials of marriage. Furthermore, as far as the theme of this book is concerned, the committed, exclusive, enduring and faithful relationship safeguards the integrity of the sexual act, both in its physical and personal characteristics. Clearly the wedding ceremony fulfils the current notion of what we understand by marriage, but in terms of morality, theology and spirituality, cohabitation can make a good case for holding its own.

In *Marriage after Modernity*[3] Thatcher writes, 'Christians who think that all preceremonial sex is wrong have wrongly assumed that the ceremonial requirement of a wedding, in fact a requirement of modernity, has always been normative. It has not. Indeed a ceremony until relatively recently has not been a requirement. The objection that cohabitation presents "a threat to the institution of marriage and the family" assumes there are fixed, not changing institutions of marriage and the family, and so, "defending" marriage entails defending a peculiar, inherited version of it.' In this book we are concerned with the integrity of sexual intercourse and cohabitation, in so far as it is a continuous, exclusive, enduring and faithful relationship, safeguards the meaning of the act. In addition to the case made in favour of cohabitation, Thatcher makes a case for a restoration of the ceremony and the pattern of relationship in betrothal as a prelude to marriage. He defines betrothal as an openness to the possibility of future marriage.

The point about cohabitation is that the widespread use of it and of marriage suggests that, while patterns of sexual behaviour have undoubtedly altered in the last 40 years, what has arisen is far from the random, occasional, promiscuous behaviour the media would have us believe. Although casual sex does indubitably take place, the overwhelming majority of sexual intercourse occurs in the context of a continuous relationship.

I am well aware that some will criticise my interpretation of cohabitation as a morality too elastic by far. I do not think so and I am in good company, if not with orthodoxy, then with thousands of ministers of all denominations, including Roman Catholics, who have pastorally adapted to the reality and the many couples who are cohabiting. If to this comes the reply that morality is not about majorities but absolutes, again I can only say that, in its wisdom, Christianity has shifted many times in deciding when a marriage is a marriage. Furthermore, Christianity cannot bury its head in the sand. It has to respond to the mammoth changes in sexuality. I would like to suggest that broadly speaking there are pre-nuptial and non-nuptial cohabitation patterns and that the former, although not the fully comprehended view of marriage and therefore in some sense incomplete, is moral. This a view with which Adrian Thatcher concurs (personal communication).

So far I have presented cohabitation in a positive light. In all fairness mention must be made of its negative aspects. Cohabitation is not always an idyllic state. As with any relationship it has its own conflict patterns. Not all cohabitations end in marriage. Some dissolve and they do so after aggression, alcoholism, gambling or extra-cohabiting affairs have taken place.

Finally, research has established that, if marriage follows two or more previous episodes of cohabitation, it may be unstable.[4] In other words those with the proclivity for multiple relationships are not made more monogamous by their cohabiting experiences.

In summary, therefore, it can be said that contemporary society does not accept total abstinence from sex before marriage. The evidence is that the solution is not promiscuous sex but rather exclusive, faithful, committed cohabitation. In my opinion, given the fluid nature of the history of Christian marriage about the time a marriage actually begins, it can accommodate cohabitation as a form of marriage. But cohabitation is not a panacea for stability and much work needs to be done to reverse the trends of divorce.

Chapter 16

Adultery

Adultery as a wrong sexual behaviour is deeply embedded in both the Old and the New Testament. In the Old Testament the origins of the transgression were to be found in the fact that, for the man, his wife's adultery might produce a child which was not his, but for whom he was materially responsible. This fear has stood the test of time and operates to this very day. Another reason why adultery was considered wrong was that in Old Testament times the wife was seen as the property of the husband and was not to be enjoyed by another man. These attitudes pass on to the New Testament where Christ condemned as adultery the remarriage of divorced persons whilst their spouse was still alive.

Today in the West marriage and marital love continue to be intimately linked with exclusive fidelity. The sexual revolution of this century has made no difference to sexual attitudes on adultery. In the survey *Sexual Behaviour in Britain* by K. Wellings et al,[1] faithfulness was considered to be the first factor of a successful marriage and was assessed by over 90 % of men and women as being very or quite important. This attitude to sex outside marriage is in contrast to the attitude to sex before marriage. In the course of the sexual revolution such practices as spouse-swapping and the freedom to have extramarital partners were freely discussed, but they never took a real hold in society.

Whilst marital faithfulness is expected, practice is different. An important study, *Adultery* by Annette Lawson,[2] found that in marriage contemporary men and women become more tolerant of sexual infidelity. Of those who remained married to the same spouse, only 50 % continued to believe that both should remain faithful, but 90 % of remarried women thought that both spouses should remain faithful. It seems, as current marriages continue, both the experience of married life and changing sexual attitudes soften expectations but equally the harsh reality of divorce stiffens the resolution to remain faithful.

The incidence of extramarital affairs varies depending on the sample tested. They range from 73 % who have had at least one adulterous relationship in Lawson's study to 3 % in Gorer's study,[3] which was carried out at an earlier period. The general consensus is that, by the age of 40, about 25–50 % of women have had one extramarital lover and about 50–65 % of men. In the United States, about 50 % of spouses had extramarital affairs.[4] All research suggests that in the last 40 years women are having more affairs than they did previously.

The number of extramarital affairs, however, differentiates men from women. 15 % of men but 25 % of women have had one affair; 40 % of men have had four liaisons but only 25 % of women have had as many.

Why do husbands and wives have affairs? There is little doubt that in general men have affairs primarily for sexual satisfaction and women for emotional satisfaction. Of course both sexes spill over into each other's territory.

Either may feel that they have no intimacy or emotional satisfaction with their spouse: they feel ignored and unrecognised for themselves; their self-esteem is gradually dropping in the marriage; they become depressed and have an affair to rediscover themselves as worthy persons who can still claim attention.

Since, in an affair, the excitement of falling in love can be recreated, it provides a powerful stimulus to the people involved. An affair offers the woman the opportunity to feel that she is still desirable. Women can discover power in their affair against the pointlessness of their marriage.[5]

In fact, the majority of extramarital affairs take place against a background of dissatisfaction with the relationship and this is particularly important for women. Dissatisfaction with marital sex is another reason.

In my clinical experience, I found that I could divide adultery into different varieties. First, there are one-night stands, which take place when the spouse is away from home for business, training or recreation. Despite the fact that one-night stands do not normally threaten the marriage, the opprobrium against one-night stands is high. This is reflected in Wellings' survey: whereas 35.8 % of men view one-night stands as wrong, 62.4 % of women do so. There is to be found in this the view that marital fidelity is an expression of mutual trust that is violated by even one act of extramarital inter-course. Ideals of monogamy seem to be held more strongly by women than by men. This gender difference has been shown to be common to many other societies. The second variety of adultery is when affairs may last from a few months to a year or two and then end, with the marriage ongoing but restructuring.

Thirdly, there is the ongoing affair in which the spouse forms a new relationship and leaves home. 'When the affair is revealed, and 80 % of men who have had an affair confess, the other spouse feels shattered, betrayed, helpless, is afraid of being abandoned and is likely to become jealous. There is a quarrel and a specific loss of trust that is hard to rebuild and even these days when sexual liberality has emerged, the sense of hurt often remains. Clinically, what is often found is the profound difference between theoretical attitudes and the harsh reality of emotional pain.'[5]

In the light of what has been written about the inner world of sexual intercourse, the severe pain of adultery can be easily understood. Men and women, particularly the latter, do not experi-ence sexual intercourse merely as a physical event. They feel it as a personal one, which conveys affirmation of the identity and sexual identity, builds self-esteem and, through the physical, gives the feeling of uniqueness to each other. There is no other signal that conveys so much to each other. When it is discovered that this unique message has been conveyed to someone else, there is a massive sense of being let down. It is not that a third party has been the beneficiary of material advantage. The real trauma is that the spouse has lost the exclusive sense of personal meaning that they held before. The persistent pain of a discovered affair is one of the strongest supports to the meaning of sexual intercourse portrayed in this book. The view of the majority of subjects studied in Wellings' survey confirms this position: 'Those seeking to promote mono-gamous and long-term relationships can be heartened by the fact that the majority view on both is that exclusivity and familiarity are more likely to lead to satisfying sex lives than short-term, multiple sexual partnerships. Half the sample agreed or agreed strongly with the statement to the effect that monogamy brings greater sexual satisfaction than having multiple partners and more than two-thirds that the quality of sexual satisfaction increases with the duration of the relationship.'

Once again the majority of men and women endorse the view that an enduring, exclusive, committed and faithful relationship is the framework for having sex. This is what Christian marriage has always said. This book inquires why this should be so, beyond the obvious procreative reason, which is no longer the reason why couples make love. Surveys show that, even without the more analytical detailed study, the view of the public inclines to affirm what I consider to be the basic sociological and psychological reasons.

Finally, what should the response to adultery be? We have the Christian answer in St John's gospel, when the Jews confront Jesus with a woman taken in adultery. Jesus responds with compassion and forgiveness, and that is the model human and Christian answer. He does not dismiss the seriousness of the act, and tells the woman to go and sin no more, but he does not condemn her. In our lives we have to do the same, but we have to go beyond compassion and forgiveness. After any act of adultery, there has to be an examination of the relationship. In conservative circles, where the right and wrong of an act is the sole order of the day and the punishment of the wrongdoer is desired, whether it is adultery or divorce, it is widely believed that there is an innocent and a guilty party. Forty years of examining human behaviour has shown me that the so-called innocent party is in actual fact rarely completely innocent. Whether it is through misunderstanding, provocation, avoidance or ineptitude, the so-called 'innocent' party is often shown to have let the 'guilty' partner down. The fashionable answer of punishing the so-called guilty is not only a passport to vengeance, but it blinds the so-called innocent partner from examining their own behaviour. This applies frequently to the adulterous man, who inevitably receives the fiercest wrath. What is often ignored is the provocation of the wife through lack of affection, sexual indifference and, nowadays, her own adultery.

The real answer is that we are all wounded people who often let each other down. There is certainly badness in humanity, but we must be very careful before we attribute the word 'bad' to a particular person. This view goes down very badly with judgemental people who want to condemn the bad. Jesus, who knew the heart of humanity, did not condemn. He must have known something of its nature to adopt such a stance.

Chapter 17

Sex and Violence

Throughout this book sexual intercourse has been set against a background of love. This love is a combination of affection and good will towards the other person. However, against the experience of love must be placed that of aggression. Freud suggested that the human personality is made up of two basic instincts: sexuality and aggression. In his schema of infantile aggression, he postulated an oral phase of taking in food at the mouth and the arrival of teeth as expression of aggression in chewing. This is the oral aggressive phase. As libido shifts to the other end of the gastrointestinal tract, to the anus, the child learns to excrete and retain faeces. This is the anal aggressive phase. Finally, there is a phallic aggressive phase. The dynamic psychology of Freud and his successors outlined a theory of the fusion between libido and aggression.

Aggression has also been explained in non-dynamic terms as part of the survival mechanism of human beings. When our survival is threatened, we are inclined to fight or flee. This pattern is seen in animals and certainly applies to human beings. Aggression is thus part and parcel of being human and is certainly linked with sexuality. Sadism is when sex and aggression fuse to get sexual pleasure out of inflicting pain; masochism, when they combine to experience sexual pleasure when receiving pain.

In its general indifference to sexuality, Christianity has not developed a philosophy about sado-masochism, and yet it should, for some have claimed that the physical suffering of Jesus and some of the martyrs and saints was nothing more than exalted masochism. But there is a world of a difference between suffering pain for a cause and enjoying pain as a source of sexual pleasure.

115

Sometimes, however, the two overlap. The practice of self-flagellation in those who are ascetic may achieve on the one hand discipline of their bodies and yet on the other experience of sexual pleasure. Certainly ignoring the subject of sado-masochism does Christianity no good because only a thorough understanding of the subtleties of the experience will unravel the difference between genuine sacrifice and excessive derivation of sexual pleasure.

Nearer our own subject of sexual intercourse, mild sado-masochistic practices are very common and Christians often do not know what to do when their partner expresses an interest in the subject. There is no doubt that some men and women enjoy mild experiences of pain and humiliation, either as a prelude to or as an accompaniment of sexual intercourse. The first thing to recognise is that, when, for example, a husband or wife wants to be spanked prior to intercourse, their partner should not be horrified. Anything that enhances sexual pleasure is part and parcel of sexual intercourse, provided it does not inflict damaging trauma or unacceptable humiliation and the partner is willing.

Sado-masochistic fantasies may also accompany sexual intercourse. Both men and women may experience fantasies of being overwhelmed, tied up, beaten or conquered as a prelude to or even in the course of making love. Once again, we must not be afraid of our fantasies, wherein reside the residue of our infantile sexual experiences and which remain part of ourselves. Both sado-masochism and fantasies are common and widespread, and Christianity has very little to say about either and yet they are part and parcel of everyday sexual life. It was thought that only men entertained them, but it is now acknowledged that women also experience them. If we see sexual intercourse as an act embedded in the divine plan of creative love, then sexual pleasure with all its varieties is welcome into the bosom of Christian spirituality.

Violence in sex and marriage

Mild to moderate sado-masochistic practices and fantasies may enhance sexual pleasure in a way that is acceptable. What is not acceptable is overt violence associated with sexual intercourse. Violence or abuse in connection with sex is often linked with men and, unfortunately, is not uncommon. Certain settings are commonly associated with violence. Drink, which acts as a suppressor of inhibitions, is often a precipitate. A man goes to a pub and drinks more than he should, returns home and wants to have sex. The setting is not that of love but of lust, by which I mean that libidinal forces alone provoke the desire for intercourse. Several things may follow. The wife can refuse to have intercourse, which inflames his desire and, from a request, his wish may become a demand. If she still refuses, then the man may become violent and hit her. Drunken violence over intercourse is very common.

Another pattern is that the man may try to make love and find himself impotent. A certain degree of inebriation results in impotence and the man becomes violent in the embarrassment of his impotence.

Yet another pattern is that a bout of inebriation may produce feelings of jealousy, and the husband may accuse the wife of not wanting to have sex with him because she is enamoured of somebody else. This produces verbal and physical abuse. If there is pre-existing tension between the couple, drink may loosen the tongue and the return home late at night and drunk may unleash recriminations that lead to violence. The setting of violence at night also accompanies the situation when an extramarital affair occurs. The aggrieved spouse uses the bedroom to attack the spouse over the affair, trying to elicit information regarding the details of how often, where, when and how sexual intercourse took place. These exchanges may be prolonged to the early hours of the morning and lead to violence.

When the marriage is in difficulties and the wife refuses intercourse, night is the time when the aggrieved husband lets out his anger and may demand sex which, if refused, leads to violence.

Psychiatric literature and practice identifies a personality disorder called psychopathic. These men and women are irritable, short-tempered and aggressive, and it does not take much to inflame them. Psychopathic personalities litter the courts with their abusive, violent behaviour and conflict over sex often triggers an outburst. In addition to psychopathy there are paranoid personalities, of which Shakespeare's Othello is an example, who are suspicious and jealous. They believe their partner is always having, or about to have, an affair. They suspect that their spouse is secretly letting them down and they examine clothing for signs of lipstick or semen as part of their conviction that they are being betrayed. Such paranoid personalities may easily turn to violence.

The point about these disturbed personalities is that, in their extreme form, they land up in psychiatric hands, but in milder forms they are very much more common and they contribute to widespread aggression in marriage. Some 30 % of men and women are subjected to violence at some point during their marriage, and very often the immediate cause is sex compounded by drink.

In traditional, idealised Christian teaching where patriarchy held sway, such violence, often perpetrated by men, was tolerated. Nowadays with the emancipation of women, this violence is found unacceptable, and rightly so. It may now lead to marital breakdown and divorce.

Rape

Sexual violence reaches its epitome in rape. The unwelcomed, coerced, enforced sexual intercourse, usually by men towards women, on the whole rare, is the fruit of power and violence gone wild. Every sexual act has a power component. In a patriarchal setting the man may feel that he is a conqueror who subdues the unruly woman. Such fantasies are widespread and intercourse is seen as a conquest. Men who rape women are often unsure of their sexual prowess, lack self-esteem, feel daunted and teased by women, and find it difficult to enter into ordinary relationships. The act of rape is more often an expression of attempted power and conquest than mere sexual pleasure. It is sometimes suggested that women who are raped have flirted and colluded with their attacker. This is very rare. Women are victims in most rape, much of which goes unreported. Rape is a total violation of what is good about sexual intercourse. There is no mutuality. The woman does not give her consent. Most of the time it takes place outside an enduring relationship and is an act of aggression. The woman as victim is humiliated, frightened and shocked, and the act leaves a trail of revulsion. It is in sexual terms an abomination.

To a lesser extent, coerced, unwelcome sexual intercourse may take place within marriage or an ongoing relationship such as cohabitation. At the heart of sexual intercourse is a voluntary, mutual desire to make love. As I have said, there are all sorts of reasons why spouses may not want to make love and their wishes must be respected. To have sexual intercourse is not a right but a benevolent mutual expression of love.

Gone are the days when the woman was seen as the property of the man whose pleasure she was there to fulfil. Christianity did contribute to such a philosophy and, even in our day and time, some men find it difficult to accept the mutuality of sexual intercourse and the right of the woman to refuse. If sexual intercourse is anything, it is an act of love freely entered into, through which pleasure and personhood are experienced and expressed. Any coercion, however small, is incompatible within this framework. All coercion and rape mobilises a feeling of anger against the perpetrator. For thousands of years women have been subjected to unwilling sex. It is the responsibility of Christianity to recognise its part in this coercion and to apologise for it.

Overall it can be seen that aggression can be an intimate component of sexuality and can range from a welcome stimulant of pleasure that is acceptable, to a totally unacceptable act of violence. Christian theology has on the whole sheltered itself from the whole area of sexuality and has no nuanced philosophy on the link between sexuality and aggression. As has been shown in this chapter, this is a pity, because it leaves countless of its adherents who experience it in its various forms without any framework of relevance within which to judge it. In its many forms – from love bites to mild sadism – it is the repertoire of ordinary sexual experiences in the home. Theology cannot afford to remain ignorant of the commonplace. It has to understand the roots of aggression, aggression's link with sexuality, and both the normality and abnormality of its various expressions.

Chapter 18

Prostitution

Prostitution is said to be the oldest profession. Certainly there are references to it in the Old Testament. The overwhelming majority of those involved are women, but there are a small number of men. The work of a prostitute excites the fantasy of successive generations, a fantasy that conveys exciting, easy, accessible sex. There is a widespread commerce in prostitution, particularly in large cities with their so-called red-light districts.

Much has been written about the life of the prostitute. Mostly it engages women who are poor, who see selling their bodies as a commercial transaction that boosts their earnings. These earnings are often given to a pimp who arranges her life and frequently exploits her. The earnings of prostitution are on the whole meagre, but a few high-class women earn a lot of money.

What is the inner motivation of the prostitute? Most studies of prostitution are carried out by sociologists who emphasise the economic and social factors of their working life. The inner world of the prostitute is rarely studied. When it is, we find women who often had an emotionally deprived upbringing, were frequently brought up in an institution and who are devoid of the feeling of being lovable. They have often, in addition, been sexually abused as children. They despise men who they view with the eye of contempt. In providing sex, they have power over men and in the exchange they stand to humiliate them. In fantasy we picture women who have frequent sex, but often these women rarely enjoy the act. They do not usually form personal relationships with their clients, although they may have their regulars. They simply have sex.

Their lives are subject to abuse, violence, the transmission of venereal disease and occasionally they are murdered. As far as the men are concerned, the prostitute is the accessible woman for intercourse that stops at orgasm. There is no personal relationship with the woman. Most men are simply seeking an orgasm.

The motives for using a prostitute are endless. There are men who have no access to women in situations such as war or being away in the navy for a long time. For these men there is a build up of libido that needs releasing. There is no thought of love or of a personal relationship. The woman is an object, a mere body. Such sexual isolation is also present in men who are loners and who cannot form relationships. Psychiatry recognises these aloof, schizoid, lonely men who cannot establish continuous relationships, indeed who are frightened of intimacy, and for whom a prostitute is a sheer physical necessity. The encounter between the psychologically isolated man and the wounded personality of the woman is in fact one of the most impoverished human exchanges. Instead of Christianity condemning this encounter, it should see in it two wounded human beings, desperately trying to get crumbs of comfort from each other – she financially, he sexually. The orgasm is the means of communication and the sad thing is that, after the orgasm, they are plunged back again into the desolate world of their isolation.

This isolation also affects some men who are not psychologically but physically deformed. They are ashamed or embarrassed about their appearance. They are afraid that no ordinary woman would have them and so they resort to the prostitute.

In addition to the variety of emotional and physical needs that motivate men to have sex with a prostitute, there are those who have special needs sexually. Again these needs are neither well known, understood nor appreciated by Christianity, which on the whole has not wanted to know the inner world of such sexuality. Sado-masochism is one of the commonest reasons for which men resort to prostitutes. Reference has already been made to the connection between sexual arousal and aggression. Although this connection affects both men and women, men are more prone to wish to express it, and so men visit prostitutes who specialise in beating, chastising or disciplining their clients. In these procedures the man regresses to the state of a child who wants to be punished. Many wives do not understand such a need or, if they do, are not prepared to act out this fantasy. The desire to be beaten or chastised has often been linked to having been beaten at school, but there is historical evidence that it predates this practice. For reasons that are not well understood, some people want to experience pain as a prelude to sexual arousal. This is a fascination which is widespread, and there are often articles in the press and features on television depicting this practice.

Some men do not wish to be beaten but want to act out their aggressive feelings on the woman and so there are prostitutes who allow themselves to be hurt. Those who defend prostitution claim that, were it not for their presence, there would be much more violence against women in society. There is no basis to prove such a view. Even with the presence of prostitution, women are still raped, beaten and sexually assaulted. The case cannot be made that prostitution acts as a shield to protect society.

After sado-masochism, there comes a whole range of fetishes. Men in particular like to have intercourse with women attired in black, in such things as silk or similar materials. They are excited by the smoothness of rubber, which is often a reminder of moments of sexual arousal when in the arms of mother. In addition, some men find women's shoes and their feet sexually arousing objects. Shoe fetishism is common. In fact, any part of the body may, in isolation, be a source of sexual excitement. Transvestites and cross-dressers may go to a prostitute to indulge their desire to dress as women and be sexually aroused by wearing female dress. Some men are aroused by women in uniform, dressed as nurses, police-women and school girls. These images too are often portrayed in the media.

Then comes the world of hospitals and medical equipment. There are prostitutes who specialise in acting as nurses giving injections and enemas. The enema was and still is a widespread legitimate orthodox therapy in many parts of the world. It is a procedure that stimulates the anus and may sexually arouse. Many adults who experienced them in childhood want to repeat them in adulthood. Rarer still is the man who may want the prostitute to urinate or defaecate over him. The link between excretion and sexuality is made in childhood and may persist in adulthood.

Thus prostitutes are used for straight sex, variations of it and also for emotional comfort. Sometimes all the man wants is to talk, to unload his feelings, seek female company and comfort. Here is a large world of frustrated and lonely men who find it difficult to have female company; a world of disappointed, hurt, lonely husbands who cannot get intimacy with their wives and who resort to prostitutes to buy female company. There are prostitutes who know this and provide a friendly, chatty interlude. Warm, caring prostitutes do exist, but most prostitutes are not 'good Samaritans'. All they want is to give sex, masturbate their client, get their money and move on to the next client. Most men who seek sexual company in the prostitute are disappointed.

Prostitution is the prime example that denies all that is written in this book. It is unsatisfactory because it is an impersonal exchange between a man and a woman. It fails to generate love. It fails to give a continuing relationship that is personal, sustaining, healing and growth promoting. Yet it has endured for thousands of years. What can we do about it? There is endless debate about making it illegal, prohibiting advertising and the establishment of ordered and supervised brothels. The discussion continues. Action is only taken when the prostitute becomes a nuisance. When attempts are made to take them off the streets altogether, they live in rooms and trade from there. If these rooms are shut, they move back onto the streets where they are less safe.

This book is not concerned with public order but with Christian answers to sexual intercourse. The more Christianity isolated sex from normality, the more men used prostitutes to gain access to it. The more Christianity made sexual intercourse unavailable, the more the prostitute was used to provide it. While there is an understandable connection between male sexual needs and prostitution that has provided for them since time began, there is no doubt that the negative attitude of Christianity towards sex has aggravated the situation. In brief, what was forbidden in one area of life was sought in another. My clinical practice has provided me with the information that every prostitute knows, namely that Christians, the married, priests and so-called devout people use prostitutes. While the traditional advocacy of self-control and discipline has its role, an even bigger role needs to be played by Christianity becoming more user-friendly to sex itself. Many married men use prostitutes because their wives have a negative attitude to sex, often conditioned by a Christian background. There is no doubt that, if both sexes, but men in particular, did not see sex as an instinctual, hedonistic perverse male pleasure but as an act of love in which God is very much present, then attitudes to sex would change.

A more benign attitude to sexuality by Christianity will move it nearer to reflecting Jesus' attitude of loving acceptance. In my book *One Like Us*,[1] I showed that Jesus, although not married, had close and warm relationships with women. He ate with sinners including prostitutes and he had a place for them in the kingdom of God.

What I am advocating is an attitude of compassion to sexual needs, forgiveness of sexual trespasses and tolerance of the unusual, because Jesus was compassionate, forgiving and tolerant.

So, for the sociologist, prostitution is the epitome of social poverty; for the feminist, the degradation of women; for the ordinary person, a combination of fascination and disgust. But for the Christian, it is the epitome of the absence of human and divine love. It is the opposite of what loving sexual intercourse should be. That is its bald meaning, namely human distortion that distills the absence of love. In so far as sexual intercourse with a prostitute is the absence of love, it should also elicit compassion for the origins of that deficiency. Christianity should work, not for condemnation, but for the long-term elimination of economic and emotional poverty that leads to prostitution. The long-term answer for Christianity is to encourage relationships of integrity, the elimination of childhood abuse, helping families with parenting, and promoting sexual education without fear and prejudices in a setting of love. The aim of Christianity is to try to help the avoidance of injury to the person in childhood, which leads to the development of personalities who embrace prostitution because they do not know what human love is.

A more favorable climate towards sexuality will enable women not only to reclaim their own sexuality, but also to understand the vulnerability of their husbands and lovers.

Sexual love must have primacy of place in Christianity in all its forms, from straight to variant sex. All of it expresses the presence of God. Just as, in my opinion, the prostitute emphasises the absence of love, so an accepting Christianity will emphasise an acceptance of God in and through sex as a powerful manifestation of love. There is no chance of an immediate change in the world of prostitution. The wounds and needs cannot alter overnight, but the incarnation set in motion a long-term healing for mankind. A change of attitude towards sex will in turn have a profound effect on prostitution.

Jesus knew that the prostitute and her client were wounded people. In the sexual act between them, he saw sin not as an expression of the badness of sex, but as the distillation of the absence of love. He dealt with the prostitute as he did with all human failure. He identified it in terms of human distortion and set in motion his life in the incarnation to rescue us. Prostitutes and their clients do not need condemnation. They need rescuing and, behind the rescuing, to see the integrity of marriage – marriage now seen not as an institution which makes sexual intercourse legal, but as something which offers the conditions for loving sexual intercourse and which protects loving human relationships.

Chapter 19

Pornography

Like prostitution, pornography has been present since ancient times. In the last 30 years or so there has been heated debate about pornography and obscenity, and what the corrupting effect, if any, might be. No consensus of opinion has emerged. It is difficult to define what pornography is. Someone expressed this confusion by saying, 'I can't describe it, but I know when I see it.' Many would agree with this view. So I will avoid definitions, which are highly subjective, and confine myself to description. Most pornography, though not all, is about the bodies of women, acts of sexual intercourse, masturbation and the enacting of sexual deviations. Nudity is one of the first factors, but nudity, although highly erotic, can also be artistically attractive. Indeed the overlap between artistic beauty and distorted bodies that are merely sexually arousing is the perennial subject of controversy. The erotic areas of the female body are the objects frequently portrayed to provide sexual arousal. They may be distorted, arranged in provocative positions, insinuating the erotic and arousing sexual excitement. This is what might be called normal pornography.

Then there is the pornography devoted to sexual deviations, pictures of sado-masochism, women being beaten or doing the beating, women tied up, women penetrated, crying for mercy. Such pornography is fantasy run riot. Pornography is widely sold, has a massive circulation and, in combination with prostitution, is a million-dollar market. Drugs, prostitution and pornography are a triad that has invaded every country and is a lucrative area of the underworld.

As with prostitution, Christianity can condemn, feel disgusted, turn away and shut its eyes to the reality. The first reality is that pornography is a common erotic arousal that may be a prelude to intercourse, masturbation, acts of sado-masochism, or to simple hedonistic sexual pleasure without any aftermath. When it is simply a visual, sexual arousal, it is an experience devoid of interpersonal content, human communication or love. It is what I understand to be an expression of lust. Sexual arousal is a prelude to sexual intercourse, which is how nature has designed it. Arousal without intercourse is a human distortion that is often pursued because sexual pleasure is sought after in its own right. Some will say, 'Why not? Isn't one of the aims of this book to restore the goodness of sexual pleasure?' Indeed it is, but the context within which sexual pleasure is experienced is what matters. Sexual arousal on its own loses its purpose. It is not that pleasure in itself is wrong, but pleasure derives its meaning from its human context of inter-personal communication. Part of my brief that I will develop at length in the final chapter is that one of the negative effects of the sexual revolution is its concomitant trivialisation of what it has put on the map. Pornography is one of the trivialisations among many. It is wrong not because it mobilises pleasure, but because it distorts the reason for sexual arousal.

One situation where pornography has a place is clinically in sexual therapy, when a man or a woman lack sexual desire or sexual drive and they may be encouraged to watch or read pornography as a way of stimulating their drive and desire to have sexual intercourse. This is an example of a therapeutic purpose.

Another use of pornography, usually by men, sometimes by women, is as an aid to masturbation. I am not dealing with mastur-bation in this book, and there is of course a whole range of settings in which masturbation takes place. In the course of my work I see the lonely, isolated, vulnerable men and women who find marriage and sexual intimacy difficult. They do not resort to prostitutes but use pornographic material to masturbate. Independent of the morality of the act, these men and women consider pornography and masturbation as a therapeutic measure. The task of the therapist is not to condemn but to help the person to move from isolated sex to sex in the context of a mutual relationship. The traditional Christian response to those with sexual difficulties was to advise marriage. We now know better and appreciate that marriage is no solution for many sexual and personal difficulties and that, even within marriage, some men and women cannot have sexual intercourse and resort to pornography and masturbation. As usual, the answer is meaningful help not moral condemnation.

Some extreme women's liberation advocates have advised women that they do not need men. All they need, it is suggested, are masturbation and pornography. Yet nature has indicated that sexual intercourse should take place in the context of heterosexual relationships (for some it will be homosexual relationships). Women have undoubtedly been exploited by men but the answer to that is not to withdraw from relationship. While some women seek solace in their fantasies and masturbate, this isolated practice does not express the pinnacle of mutual sexual fulfilment.

Beyond sexual arousal and masturbation, pornography, i.e. magazines that portray many sexual variations, has wide sales. Those fascinated by such variations find satisfaction in luxuriating over their contents. The most worrying are those that portray sadism. Do these magazines corrupt? From time to time horrifying sadistic crimes are committed and the homes of the perpetrators are found to be full of the relevant journals. The media make an obvious association and the public accepts the link. The link is actually not so obvious. An association by itself is not a cause and effect relationship. By and large, it is believed that the few sadistic killers who are found with these magazines, are first and foremost sadistic in their personality and they collect such magazines as a consequence. It takes more than a magazine to transform an ordinary person into a sadistic killer. What is possible is that the media and magazines may offer an example that is then copied by a person disposed to this behaviour.

Another group of sexual variations involve paedophilic tendencies. In recent times, rings of paedophiles and their accompanying friends have been discovered. Society finds the paedophile particularly disturbing. There is no doubt that paedophilia is a totally unacceptable behaviour and it is difficult to elicit sympathy and compassion for such men and women. In fact, they are really disturbed people and, although their disturbance does not excuse their behaviour, very often they are lonely, isolated and immature. They need treatment, although it is easier to say this than for them to get it. Sexual aberrations are very difficult to treat and such people are often just locked up.

I have described the range of pornography, from its common use of sexual arousal to its more specialised exhibition of sexual variations. Next we examine the highly debatable question of what is art and what is pornography. This is a debate that has no conclusion because tastes differ. Nevertheless, I am concerned to show that there is a difference. Here are some of the points to be considered.

The first point to be acknowledged is that the body, and the naked body in particular, is beautiful. It is beautiful in its natural setting and in its erotic potential. Nudity may both distort and enhance this beauty. Its perennial presentation in magazines and pictures and its wide use to sell goods are constant reminders of its universal attraction. The Christian must judge the presentation of the body by aesthetic and artistic criteria and not through prejudice. When sex is not approved of in general in any form, then its pictorial manifestation will be condemned. If the view of this book is taken that sex is one of the most important divine gifts, then appreciation of the body is something to be relished. What is to be relished is its beauty, not its covert erotic message alone. The two are intricately mixed. The body as an erotic entity is attractive but only when set in the context of human integrity. It is not for me to set out criteria of artistic integrity. I am merely saying that it is these criteria that matter, not sexual prejudices.

The context of beauty is one criterion. The next is the setting of the erotic portrayal. We are accustomed to place erotic beauty in museums, exhibitions and even in the sanctity of the home. These places confer a degree of respectability. The setting is not the only passport of respectability. The artistic portrayal is another. Greek and Roman nudes and contemporary art clearly exhibit character-istics that differentiate them from the crude portrayal in underground erotic literature. Pornography in the latter setting is crude, monotonous, repetitive and, as in poor literature, it bores because it portrays sex without the rich human context of personal dilemmas, conflicts and interaction. In other words, crude por-nography is not wholly human. It devalues human sexuality.

Another criterion of the genuine exhibition of the erotic is whether it is associated with or portrays human love, which in turn portrays divine love. I have already quoted the Song of Songs. It portrays human beauty, both male and female, and is not embarrassed to draw the conclusion that it is admired, sexually exciting and deeply appreciated. All this physical beauty has a divine stamp on it. It reflects the image of its creator. The poem is aware that the erotic excites and perturbs, but the excitement displayed here is not merely genital. It involves the whole person in the crisis of love and death. It affirms the thesis of this book that sexuality mobilises love that involves the whole person.

So at the conclusion of this chapter we can restate the chief points that distinguish art from pornography. Real erotic art portrays artistic integrity; in other words it does not distort physical beauty. It mobilises the creative involvement of the whole person, not merely the genitals. It evokes admiration for the body. Art is set in the context of the real person. Pornography narrows down the focus to the area of mere genital arousal. For men, breasts, buttocks and thighs excite, but real sexual involvement engages the whole person in a setting of real life. The woman who arouses is capable of involving feelings of interest, sympathy and empathy, not merely sexual titillation. Finally, pornography is not set in the context of love. As we have seen in this book, to be real sexuality engages another person in a personal and interpersonal context of love. Pornography is not designed to do that. Most of the time it merely titillates visually, although there is pornographic material that arouses the senses.

These observations do not exhaust the differentiation between erotic art and pornography, but they give us clues as to how this might be done. Christians must insist that the body is a source of wonder and a vehicle of divine love. The proper response is to celebrate the wonder and to participate in the love.

Part IV

Challenges for the Contemporary Church

Chapter 20

Contraception

For the overwhelming majority of Christians contraception is not a problem. It has been accepted by the Anglican Church for over 70 years and for nearly every Christian it is taken as the norm. Even large numbers of Roman Catholics have accepted it. As with cohabitation, many Catholic priests have adapted to its presence pastorally. So why devote a chapter to it?

First of all, because I care for the integrity of the Roman Catholic Church. It is a great Church with a long tradition of teaching the truth, and at the present moment its teaching on contraception is a weak link in its moral authority. Even more importantly, combining the condemnation of contraception with that of abortion and divorce dilutes the enormous moral wrong of the latter two. Forty years of studying and counselling marital problems have left me in no doubt that the leading moral challenge of our time is marital breakdown, not contraception. Finally, I feel uncomfortable with a Church I love peddling with excuses that masquerade as truth when it is defending its stance on contraception. The integrity of the truth matters enormously and, if the Church is to be taken seriously, it must get its teaching on contraception right.

There is also the question of evangelisation. While the majority of young people in practice ignore this teaching, their faith is undermined when they are expected to believe in something that makes no sense to them. Furthermore, in schools Catholic teachers have a hard enough job to educate for sexual morality. If they are lumbered with an orthodoxy about contraception that they are often ignoring in their own lives, the task becomes virtually impossible.

At the present moment the Roman Catholic Church is involved

in a conspiracy of silence with regard to contraception. The Magisterium reiterates and few listen. Theologians do not dare to explore what many do not believe. The world quietly ignores the Church in this matter and, by believing it is wrong in this respect, also ignores its teaching on abortion and divorce, which is very sad. So in this chapter I return to the history of contraception, its recent history and the reasons why the teaching is not tenable. I also pay attention to its defenders and finally I will make my own position clear.

Those who want to study the history of the treatment of contraception in the tradition of the Church should refer to the classic study by John T. Noonan Jnr[1] to which, like so many others, I owe a great deal. The first few chapters set the scene in understanding the attitude to contraception. A combination of the Stoic indifference to sexual pleasure embraced by early Christians, coupled with the affirmation of virginity, set the scene for the conviction that procreation was the only justification for sexual intercourse.

Morally, contraception was seen as either impeding new life, therefore going against the purpose of intercourse, or killing the possibility of life. Augustine and Jerome proclaimed the duality. Augustine was of course infinitely more influential. Sexual intercourse was permitted for procreation and, secondarily, to satisfy concupiscence and to avoid adultery. The main position to emerge from Augustine is that coitus is for procreation.

This view was reinforced in the Middle Ages and, although subtle nuances of accepting pleasure and underlining the need to avoid adultery were introduced, the primacy of procreation was not challenged.

Coming to modern times, tradition – what was available in the moral law books – understood sexual intercourse to be for the purposes of procreation and the remedy of concupiscence. Canon law, as defined in its version of 1917–18, concluded that sexual intercourse was for procreation, mutual help and the remedy of concupiscence. These purposes are the language of the meaning of marriage in terms of the primary ends – the procreation and education of children, and the secondary ends – mutual help and the relief of concupiscence.

In 1930 the Anglican Church accepted contraception. It did not provide a philosophy for sexual intercourse, but merely accepted it as Luther had done the marriage of priests. Pius XI replied with his encyclical *Casti Connubii*, in which he condemned contraception afresh. He extended the meaning of sexual intercourse to pro-creation, mutual help and a remedy for concupiscence or sexual desire, but also included for the first time mutual love.

In 1951 Pius XII made the historic acceptance of birth regulation by the use of the infertile period. So birth regulation entered the mind of the Catholic Church. In addition, his teaching reiterated that sexual intercourse was for procreation, mutual help, the relief of concupiscence and now added the validity of moderate pleasure. At the Second Vatican Council, there was a genuine revolution of teaching on marriage and sexual intercourse. Those who cannot see how the Church can change its teaching on contraception are ignorant of the historic changes adopted by the Council, which were revolutionary. The Council dropped the language of primary and secondary ends and its understanding of marriage as a contract, and saw it instead as a covenant relationship. Above all, it under-stood marriage and sexual intercourse in terms of love, love that was human, total, faithful and exclusive. It also endorsed responsible parenthood, that is to say parents have the responsibility of limiting the size of their family to what they can cope with economically, socially and emotionally. The Council left the means of limiting the family for further study.

Among the many reasons for writing this book is that the Council, helped by the Holy Spirit, came to the conclusion that love is at the centre of Christian marriage and of sexual intercourse. It left to the people of God to explore the meaning of this love. Unfortunately, this never took place because the encyclical *Humanae Vitae* put an end to the exploration of sexuality. The Church has been obsessed with promulgating the prohibition of contraception against its people who have not received its teaching and a world that has ignored it.

After the Council, Paul VI appointed a commission to advise him, which it did in due course, and its majority recommendation was in favour of accepting contraception. But Paul VI did not accept this advice. Lest anyone thinks that I am challenging the Petrine office by refusing to accept his right to issue an encyclical that was based on his own authority, let me say at once that I do accept that right. I also note this because for some, *Humanae Vitae* is of no interest as a document that examines sexuality but rather as a document that concerns obedience to authority. Many who are rattled by the refusal to accept it are anxious because, unconsciously, their security is threatened. I am primarily concerned with sexual truth.

In 1968 *Humanae Vitae* was issued in which sexual intercourse is understood to have a procreative and unitive meaning. Specifically, *Humanae Vitae* 12 stated that 'each and every marriage act (sexual intercourse) must remain open to the transmission of life'. I have no quarrel with every act of sexual intercourse being open to the unity of the couple, but I cannot accept that every act of sexual intercourse must remain open to the transmission of life. Why not?

I cannot accept this simply because the design from nature denies the possibility. It is clear that fertilisation can only occur when an ovum and a sperm unite. The sperm does not produce life alone. This is only possible at the most for five days in each of the woman's monthly cycles. Therefore what God says is that procreation is not possible in every act of sexual intercourse. The woman is not always open to new life. The idea of sexual intercourse being open to new life is a very male-orientated view.

Clearly the tradition that Paul VI wished to preserve was to safe-guard procreation. But this can be done by treating the whole period of fertility from puberty to menopause as a possibility for new life. Openness to new life in every act of sexual intercourse is a meaning-less human contradiction. Openness to loving unity for every act is a reality and Paul VI was absolutely correct in that respect.

Another way of looking at the Church's position, strongly reinforced by John Paul II's teaching of the theology of the body, is that the latter is a generative reality and that each act of sexual intercourse has both a unitive and a procreative potential by the very nature of the encounter between the sexes. The integrity or goodness of coitus must respect both aspects. This is very much the view of John Paul II and he was influential in the production of *Humanae Vitae*. I would accept that the male and female have a generative potential (with the caveat of the limitations in the woman) but I would argue that nowhere in the Scriptures, or in natural law thinking, is there a clear indication that this potential must be activated in every act of sexual intercourse. The generative potential of the body, that generative self-communication of which John Paul II speaks, belongs to the total life span of the couple. As I said before, the design of nature denies that every act is potentially procreative. The totality of married life is procreative, but not every act. What the Church teaches, namely the indissolubility of the unitive and the procreative, is a conclusion drawn to support the teaching on contraception but which is nowhere to be found in the physical and psychological reality of intercourse. In fact, we can see that biology and love are not inherently united from the course of events after the menopause, where love continues in intercourse but procreation ceases.

Furthermore, it could be argued that men and women have been given the freedom and control over nature to select the moment of procreation. In other words, whereas every sexual act is open to its loving components, the responsibility of new life is so great and important that it is up to the parents to choose the occasion to bring it into operation. The Church accepts that the couple have the moral right to decide the size of their family. Equally, given the generative nature of the body, they have the moral freedom and right to exercise the moment of its implementation.

To sum up, the Church teaches that every act of sexual intercourse is by design procreative and loving and, even if the procreative potential is limited to a few days, it must not be disrupted. There is neither Scriptural nor natural law evidence to support this thesis. Paul VI and John Paul II claim that this thesis is self-evident and expect the world to see it, but this has not come about. I think what the Church is trying to say is that every encounter between a man and a woman is life-giving in the widest sense of the word, and it always remains so, while on a few occasions it is life-giving in the biological sense.

In *Humanae Vitae* 13 we read 'Men rightly observe that to force the use of marriage on one's partner without regard to his or her condition or personal and reasonable wishes in the matter, is no true act of love, and therefore offends the moral order in its particular application to the intimate relationship of husband and wife. If they reflect further, they must also recognise that an act of mutual love which impedes the capacity to transmit life which God the Creator, through specific laws, has built into it, frustrates his design which constitutes the norms of marriage, and contradicts the will of the Author of life.' Clearly Paul VI in writing this had a morality of natural law in mind. Men and women, both Catholic and non-Catholic, have considered his words and, using their reason, cannot see their justification because, as I have clearly pointed out, the laws of God on procreation are not as described in the encyclical. Every act is not open and cannot be open to procreation. The whole of marriage is open to procreation.

Given that the Catholic Church accepts birth regulation, young people and indeed most people cannot understand what is the difference between using the infertile days and using contraception. The orthodox answer is that the infertile days do not impede the possibility of fertilisation. Young people return with the argument that nowhere in the Scriptures or in natural law does God say that every possibility of fertilisation must be respected. What God has put into human design is the possibility of fertilisation which has a span of 40 years to be realised.

We move on to paragraph 17 of *Humanae Vitae* 13: 'Responsible men can become more deeply convinced of the truth of the doctrine laid down by the Church on this issue if they reflect on the consequences of methods and plans for the artificial restriction of increases in the birth rate.' We have seen that reasonable and responsible human beings cannot see the essential reasoning behind the teaching. What about the consequences? The paragraph then goes on to suggest that marital infidelity and a general lowering of moral standards will ensue and, especially, that the young will be tempted by the presence of contraception. This is a favourite argument of those who perceive the present situation of sexual intercourse as moral chaos and proclaim the wisdom of the encyclical.

First of all, let us look at the incidence of extramarital activity. Behind the Pope's fears is the view of adultery as mainly entailing lust perpetrated by men. This is not so. Adultery certainly has a physical basis but also an emotional constituent. Here it accurately reflects an outlet from a complex frustration in the married state. There is a fantasy that in their natural state men and women would run riot with their sexual urges and that contraception would facilitate these urges. Any real understanding of human nature accepts human weakness but also recognises sexual integrity. Adultery is as old as human nature and existed before the widespread use of modern contraception. But has it increased in the era of widespread contraception? Let us turn to the one confident source of data. Kinsey[2] collected his material in the forties before widespread contraception had arrived. This is what he had to say on extramarital sexual intercourse: 'On the basis of these active data, and allowing for the cover-up that has been involved, it is probably safe to suggest that about half of all married males have intercourse with women other than their wives, at some time while they are married.' This figure of 50 % suggests that adultery in our day and time is no more in evidence than in the forties in the United States.

It is not true to say that ordinary men and women adopt the attitude, 'Oh good, we have contraception. Let us see with whom we can have an extramarital affair.' The reality is, as I have said before, that multiple and complex factors in the marriage lead to the need to look elsewhere. If Christianity is to do its homework towards sexual and marital morality, it should pay attention to the inner world of the dynamics of marriage. Centuries of a simplistic view about the temptation of sex have blinded us to the fact that marriage is more than a response to mere concupiscence. It involves human love, and understanding how that love unfolds is the key answer to sexual fidelity. It is true that, as the Pope says, men and women and the young need incentives to keep the moral law. As far as the married are concerned, the incentive is the integrity of marriage.

But what of the young? The same answer applies. The young do not say, 'We have contraceptives. Let us use them to have sex.' First of all, we must ask whether there is more sex among the young. Nobody would deny that there is. I have quoted figures showing there is more sex among the young and earlier involvement in sexual activity. Is this merely due to the advent of contraception? Those who oppose contraception will naturally say so, but the answer is far more complex. The young have to be divided into those under and over the age of 16. Starting with those under 16, this century has seen a lowering of the age of puberty through good health and nutrition. Nobody would want to stop these as a means of keeping young people sexually inactive. There is an erotic bombardment and a sexual revolution which create an increasing pressure to have sexual intercourse. In addition, there are a host of personal reasons which I described in Chapter 14. These are curiosity, opportunity, peer pressure, the desire not to be left behind, being in a relationship, fear of losing boy or girl friend, the need to feel loved and the association of sex with love and alcohol.

In an age where the Churches have lost touch with their young and blind obedience to authority is a thing of the past, the prohibition of contraception is no answer to teenage sexuality. The answer is sex education that is about relating sex to love and, in an age where the simple answer of linking sex to procreation no longer persuades, the link to love is the only answer. Whenever I talk to school pupils about sex, I link it to love and they respond. The prohibition of contraception as a prelude to understanding the meaning of sex is irrelevant. Finally, what must be said is that sexual intercourse under the age of 16 is not only prohibited by law, but it also has little chance to connect with mature love. The answer is to spell out what mature love is as far as it is possible.

The other danger with sexual intercourse under the age of 16 is pregnancy. No child should be brought into the world under these circumstances, and when it happens it is a tragedy. Sex education is the first line of prevention against intercourse and pregnancy. Contraception is another answer. This view horrifies the orthodox. In their eyes it compounds one immorality with another. It is clear that sexual intercourse under the age of 16 should not take place. As part of public policy, education should aim to avoid this. Education, coupled with contraception, is the answer. The answer is certainly not abortion, but the criticism against abortion would be much stronger if the Catholic Church offered an informed and meaningful sexual education, and accepted contraception.

Sexual intercourse between those over the age of 16, which of course is much more common, is often associated with prophesies of doom and gloom. In fact, in this age group, there is no moral chaos, as the overwhelming majority of couples have intercourse in the setting of cohabitation, as described in Chapter 15. What I want to say here is that the research evidence suggests that, by and large, premarital sexual intercourse does not occur in a setting of moral chaos of fleeting, casual, promiscuous sex. Most of it, but not all, takes place within the confines of love, which the Second Vatican Council described as human, total, faithful and exclusive. In cohabitation, sex often conforms to these criteria. Critics will say that I am denying the reality that they see and read in the media. In fact, what is presented there is often the sexual fantasy, most often of men, of how they believe human beings should behave.

Returning to the encyclical, it says: 'Another effect that gives us cause for alarm is that a man who grows accustomed to the use of contraceptive methods may forget the reverence due to a woman, and, disregarding her physical and emotional equilibrium, reduce her to a mere instrument for the satisfaction of his own desires, no longer considering her as his partner whom he should surround with care and affection.' The sentiments here are fine, but what about the reality? First, historical reality: it is ironic that a Church, indeed Christianity as a whole, which is steeped in patriarchy and the humiliation and violation of women throughout its history, should now be concerned with the dignity of women. But in fact, is there any evidence that women feel or are abused through the use of contraceptives?

What is forgotten is that the modern woman has the right, ability and capacity to say 'no' when she does not want to have intercourse, with or without contraceptives. What is totally omitted in this androcentric passage is the boon that contraception has been for women. Men do not appreciate the anxiety women felt at the thought of being pregnant yet again, and how this anxiety terrorised their lives and spoilt their sexual satisfaction. The ability to control conception is one of the great advances of our age. This encyclical would have been differently influenced if it had been written by a woman. It is not as if the Church does not appreciate the need to control the number of births. In its attempt to defend the impossible, this passage portrays a situation for which, by and large, there is no evidence. If there was, it is the fault of the Church for not defending the power and the right of women to simply say 'no' to a man when they feel their dignity is being compromised.

Finally, the Pope describes the situations where governments or public authorities compel couples to use contraceptives to avoid national family problems. There is real danger in this possibility.

China, for instance, restricts family size. What the Pope disregards is the common sense of people. Governments have limited authority to impose patterns of private human behaviour. India tried it, and the government was defeated. Thirty years after its promulgation and after nearly a century of widespread contraception, there is no evidence of this danger appearing on the horizon. The attempt by governments to manipulate personal behaviour is complex. In dictatorships it is slightly easier; in democracies it is much more difficult. It is society that has greater power to manipulate. The Pope should have been much more concerned with the media which sells the trivialisation of sex, not contraception.

The failure of any convincing argument in favour of this teaching for nearly 30 years has led its defenders to claim that it is prophetic. In so far as the dangers warned of in the encyclical, sexual intercourse has not led to chaos, governments have not gone mad. In fact, contraception has reduced the anxieties of women. It has given control over conception to mankind and is a magnificent example of the power that God has given to the world over creation. I have no doubt that there are cases where contraception has been abused, but on the whole its advantages largely outweigh its disadvantages.

What about my personal position as a Roman Catholic taking this stance against the encyclical? From time to time I receive letters from those who are shocked by my position, heavily outweighed, I must say, by those in favour of what I say. But I must justify my position. This I do by returning to the Second Vatican Council's *Declaration on the Laity*, in the section on the Church: 'An individual layman, by reason of the knowledge, competence or outstanding ability which he may enjoy, is permitted and sometimes even obliged to express his opinion on things that concern the good of the Church. When occasions arise, let this be done through the agencies set up by the Church for this purpose. Let it always be done in truth, in courage, and in prudence, with reverence and charity towards those who by reason of their sacred office represent the person of Christ.'[3] I have examined my conscience and believe that I have complied with this instruction. My conscience, which is well informed, tells me that this teaching cannot be sustained by reason and cannot be found in the Scriptures. By maintaining its stance, the Church is inflicting a wound on itself and dilutes its authority on such matters as abortion and divorce. Incidentally, in their desperate attempts to support this teaching, its advocates claim that contraception is a cause of marital breakdown. In my 40 years of investigating and working on the problems of marital breakdown, I find no evidence in the literature or in practice for such a connection.

I believe that, in terms of theology, the people of God have been given, but have not received, this teaching. While the majority of Roman Catholics ignore this teaching, this situation is not good for the Roman Catholic Church because, as I repeat, it dilutes its authority.

The fervent adherents to this teaching are really shocked at the possibility of change. How can the Church with the aid of the Holy Spirit get it wrong? If it has got it wrong, what about other matters such as abortion, homosexuality and so on? It is important to appreciate that the authority of the Church, given by Jesus, derives its strength from teaching the truth. There is enormous evidence that over the course of time the Church has changed its teaching on marriage and the meaning of sexual intercourse. The Roman Catholic Church has endured for 2,000 years for many reasons, one of which is its flexibility to recognise emerging truths and to adapt to them. Recent examples are the way it jettisoned the traditional language over the ends of marriage and substituted love as its main foundation. Changing its teaching on contraception is a small matter compared to what it achieved at the Council. Historically, it has faced issues such as slavery, usury and a host of moral problems. For me, changing its teaching on contraception is not only possible, it is essential. Sooner or later it has to be done.

But I want to conclude on a different note. The greatest Christian value is love. God is love. The Second Vatican Council made enormous strides in developing a personalistic morality over marriage and sex. *Humanae Vitae* put a stop to this development, which I personally consider a tragedy.

The reason why I have written this book is to advance our understanding of human, personal, sexual love, and to confront the world with Christian values. The Church has believed that, by defending the encyclical in the last 20 years, it has promoted Christian values. I think in this matter the Church is respected for its teaching, but not for the contents of the encyclical. It is a Church that does not give up easily but in my opinion it should have respect for the truth. There are some among my critics who say, 'How do you know what you say is true? Why should we accept your word against the teaching authority of the Church?' My answer is that in sexual matters, the Church has a tradition that has left a trail of misleading, misjudging and misunderstanding human experience. Its attitude on sex, sexual pleasure and women needs a lot of correcting, and in truth much correction has taken place. It is only in this century with the aid of psychology that we have the means of a deeper discovery of the truth. This truth belongs to the whole people of God, and their experience has rejected the teaching of this encyclical. What I am ultimately relying on is not only my knowledge and the knowledge of the psychological sciences, but also the truth experienced by the overwhelming majority of people and the wisdom of the ecumenical stance on this subject. I would shout with delight in the presence of one compelling argument in favour of the encyclical. I have waited in vain so far. The world desperately needs truth, and we cannot wait for ever.

Chapter 21

Married Clergy

In *Europe without Priests*,[1] Jan Kerkhofs writes in the introduction:
'It is well known that, with few exceptions, the Catholic faith communities outside Europe and North America have been confronted
with a chronic shortage of priests. What is new is the fact that in
the Western world, too, the average age of priests is rapidly
increasing; that the number of candidates for the priesthood in
dioceses and the religious orders is continuing to decline or is
stagnant at a very low level and that more and more parishes no
longer have a priest who is resident locally.' He then goes on to
give facts and figures of this decline and to suggest remedies. One
suggestion is the ordination of married priests, and this chapter is
devoted to the subject.

The biblical basis for celibacy is to be found in the teaching of
Jesus: 'The disciples said to him, "If that is how things are between
husband and wife, it is not advisable to marry." But he replied, "It
is not everyone who can accept what I have said, but only those to
whom it is granted. There are eunuchs born that way from their
mother's womb, there are eunuchs made so by men and there are
eunuchs who have made themselves that way for the sake of the
kingdom of heaven. Let anyone accept this who can"' (Matt.
19:10–12). Here Jesus introduced the single state dedicated to God.
What is often forgotten is the last sentence. Jesus knows that celibacy
is hard and he does not impose it on anyone. He elicits a voluntary
response.

Again we find in Mark: 'Jesus said, "I tell you solemnly, there is
no one who has left house, brothers, sisters, father, children or land
for my sake and for the sake of the gospel who will not be repaid a

hundred times over houses, brothers, sisters, mothers, children and land – not without persecutions – now in this present time and, in the world to come, eternal life"' (Mark 10:29–31).

In Luke we find: 'Then Peter said, "What about us? We left all we had to follow you." He said to them "I tell you solemnly, there is no one who has left house, wife, brothers, parents or children for the sake of the kingdom of God who will not be given repayment many times over in this present time and, in the world to come, eternal life"' (Luke 18:28–30). Paul wished all men to be in the same state as himself (1 Cor. 7:7): 'An unmarried man can devote himself to the Lord's affairs . . . but a married man . . . is torn two ways' (1 Cor. 7:32).

These texts, however, do not link celibacy directly to the priestly ministry. In early Christianity, they were connected with baptism, and anyone could follow them. Celibacy as the duty of the priestly state was introduced only gradually, and it reflected in the early centuries the high values attached to virginity and the life of ascetics and monks. The gradual evolution of celibacy took place against a background of an uncompromising rejection of sexuality. All sexual activity, even within marriage for the sake of procreation, was frowned upon. As noted in the earlier chapters, human sexuality was not seen as a precious gift from God. Porter shows how the demand for a sexually chaste priesthood for reasons of cultic purity demonstrated and promoted this standard powerfully.[2]

Thus, by the first decade of the fourth century, at the local Synod of Elvira held in Spain, Canon 33 required all clergy to abstain totally from their wives and not to beget children. It was not celibacy, non-marriage, that was required, but abstention from sex within marriage. It was a prohibition made in the interests of cultic purity. The Canons of Elvira, taken together, single out the clergy from the laity in the promotion of a clerical elite based on sexual asceticism.

The first attempt to impose clerical celibacy as a universal law came some 60 years later in a papal decretal under Pope Sincius in 385. The insistence on the clergy avoiding marriage stemmed from an interpretation that virginity, as the higher lifestyle, was the only fitting one for the Christian priesthood. According to Porter, most twentieth-century scholars have argued that the driving motive for the single state of the priesthood was cultic purity: 'He who stands at the altar must keep himself away from the sexual act.'

The underlying fear of women is ever present. Only men who abstained from women were considered pure enough to handle the body and blood of Christ, were sufficiently set apart from the laity to lead the Church and were holy enough to maintain strict morality.

Nevertheless what prevailed from the fourth to the eleventh century was a position in which the clergy were married but were supposed to remain continent. This clash between the ideal and reality defeated many, as it continues to defeat them today. The Gregorian reforms issued in 1059, 1063 and 1074 ordered the faithful to avoid attending masses celebrated by priests who had sexual relations with their wives. Finally, the Second Lateran Council of 1139 declared that clerical marriage was invalid. This rule has remained to this very day in the Roman Catholic Church. At the Reformation Luther allowed clerical marriage. Companionship, mutual support and even procreation were not the main reasons for this step. For Luther, fallen human nature was susceptible to sexual temptation and, because he saw many Catholic clergy in his day violating their celibate vows, he took the view that everybody, including the clergy, needed a sexual outlet. Human nature for him was diseased, and the marriage of the clergy was a hospital for the remedy of this state. There was here no appreciation of the goodness of sex. Just as in the 1930s the Anglican Church adopted birth control as a pragmatic measure, so at the Reformation Luther similarly accepted clerical marriage. So, to this very day, the reformed churches allow their clergy to marry as do the Eastern churches. The Roman Catholic Church stands alone amongst the major Christian denominations in insisting on clerical celibacy. But what is the reality?

For the most comprehensive treatment of Catholic clergy from the point of view of their continence, the work of A. W. R. Sipe stands out.[3] In his study of 1,500 priests, he found 2 % who really achieved celibacy, 8 % who consolidated celibate practice and 40 % who remain celibate. The other 50 % broke their celibacy in some way or another. In my clinical practice I have seen many priests who have had sexual relationships with women, have become sexually involved with children, have turned to alcohol or who are extremely lonely. In other words, my work and that of Sipe confirms that, as in most of the history of celibacy, there is a large component of those who undertake it but cannot keep it. Hardly a week passes without some story of a priest being charged with sexual abuse. I am not saying that Catholic priests are more likely to abuse children sexually. What I am saying is that now that society is more aware of sexual abuse, priests, who were always privileged before, are no longer so.

The infringement of celibacy is one of the indications of the difficulties of priesthood. The reduction of numbers entering the seminaries in the last 30 or 40 years is another, a time which coincides with the sexual revolution. I do not think the association is accidental. For the first time in history in the West, we have an understanding of sexuality as an intrinsic part of the human personality. In this century sexuality is no longer seen as a disease, as an expression of human frailty, but as a normal component of the human personality.

This revolution has undoubtedly influenced Christianity, and in the course of this book I have referred to studies which show the evolution of Christianity towards sexuality.[4] In these studies we see the attitude of the Churches, including the Roman Catholic Church. It is a response of gradual acceptance of the precious gift of God. This acceptance is linked with love, the principal characteristic of Christianity. In my view, the case to be made for a Catholic married clergy is not primarily a fall in numbers. I put forward the case that there is a God-appointed time to allow for those who want to enter a married clergy.

We have seen in this book a view of sexuality that from the first centuries is distorted. The link of celibacy with the clergy was a cultic relationship based on the fear of women and sex. This fear of women and sex has no foundation in truth. Christianity has done a massive injustice to sexuality. There is no essential connection between celibacy and priesthood. It is based on a false link. Nor can we concede any longer the fact of married clergy in the light of Luther's idea that marriage is a hospital for the sexually wounded. Marriage, as I have tried to show, provides the appropriate conditions for the integrity of sexual intercourse, now seen as fostering love. In sexual intercourse the married priest enacts a sacred liturgy of love, that, far from alienating him from the sacrifice of the mass, brings the two liturgies of love together. Sexual intercourse, as showing the sections on spirituality, gives direct access to the life of the Trinity itself and to a pool of spirituality that is really rich.

Marriage of the clergy is indicated in Scripture. In Timothy, we find: 'Here is a saying that you can rely on: To want to be a presiding elder is to want to do a noble work. That is why the president must have an impeccable character. He must not have been married more than once, and he must be temperate, discreet and courteous, hospitable and a good teacher; not a heavy drinker, nor hot-tempered, but kind and peaceable. He must not be a lover of money. He must be a man who manages his own family well and brings his children up to obey him and be well-behaved' (1 Tim. 3:1–5). Similarly, deacons must be husband of one wife. The same instruction is given in Titus 1:6. Here in these passages we find the earliest views of pastoral practice before the distortion on sexuality took hold in the early centuries. If one thinks of the characteristics of proper behaviour desired, they are infinitely more important than celibacy. I might be criticised for choosing these passages in prefer-ence to the words of Jesus and Paul in favour of the single state. I have no objection to the single state linked to ordination as an expression of service. I do have great objection to the advocacy of the single state as a denial of the goodness of sex. What I am really saying is that celibacy should be voluntary. This is not a novel idea, but it reflects more accurately the words of Jesus. Here, as everywhere, Jesus invites, he does not demand.

It is now recognised that some women wish to be ordained, but I am not dealing here with this topic. I confine myself to men who want to be priests but do not want to be celibate. The case I am making is that to ordain married priests is not a concession to the frailty of sexuality, but a recognition of its divine wonder. A married priest can give a lead to the goodness of marriage and, being familiar with the inner world of marriage, can handle the needs of the married more effectively.

Just as in the case of contraception, so in the case of married clergy, the Roman Catholic Church is faced with a reassessment of its tradition. In the case of celibate clergy, it has more support from Scripture, but Scripture does not make a compulsory connection between celibacy and ordination. This link is more in keeping with the negativity towards sexuality than any affirmation of the goodness of the single state. The Church needs to move forward to embrace the goodness of sexuality. In changing its attitude to contraception and celibacy for the clergy, it will take a leap forward in the celebration of sexuality, two steps which are urgent and essential.

Chapter 22

The Single State

I grew up in the Catholic Church that was full of single people dedicated to God as priests, nuns and the religious. Now entry into all these forms of religious life is reduced. In addition, there were a minority of single men and women whose status was not clear.

In the previous chapter, I referred to Jesus' statement on being a eunuch for the kingdom of God. There is no doubt that such a state has a genuine place in Christianity. As far as we know Jesus himself was a single person. In my psychological study of Jesus,[1] I wrote that the single state of Jesus was not a criticism of marriage. He had, after all, worked his first miracle at the wedding feast at Cana. Rather, I attributed his single state to the fact that, as Saviour of the world, he could not confine himself to another person exclusively. His life was one of complete availability.

The single person may channel his or her love in the same way to everyone. It is hard to exaggerate what the Church and civilisation owe to this generosity of love. Through the presence of monasteries, wisdom, literature and art were preserved in the dark ages. The scholarship in the monasteries was a prelude to the flowering of the universities where the religious became eminent teachers. Beyond education, hospitality was another sign of the monastery and convent, and, in the harsh days of old, pilgrims and travellers needing food and shelter found them in these religious houses.

In our own age, Catholics and others owe a great deal to the sisters and brothers who offered their whole life to the education of children. It is fashionable nowadays to criticise this education. Certainly from the point of view of this book, sexual education and the teaching of sexual morality were not always handled in the best possible way. Beyond education there was the care of the sick and nursing was another area where sisters and brothers excelled. They offered a service that ultimately saw the patient as another Christ and went beyond the technicalities to love the whole person. They looked after the elderly long before it was fashionable for the secular world to do so. This care also extended to the poor and the deprived. Mother Teresa is a modern example, looking after the poor and dying in India. Side by side with the poor are the emotionally deprived, orphans, pregnant women and the mentally ill, all of whom have been subjects of care.

The single person has also been pre-eminent in missionary work. The presence of Christianity in Africa, Asia and elsewhere owes much to priests and nuns. These men and women offered their lives in far away lands, and sustained physical and mental illness for the sake of Christ. They were and are pioneers in evangelisation to whom the Church owes a great deal.

Much of the work in education, nursing and work for the deprived has now been taken over by the state in Western societies, but the torch was lit by the religious.

All I have described is the work of the active orders. In addition, there are the enclosed orders where, day in day out, worship and prayer continue. These beacons of prayer are vital for the life of the Church. They are a constant reminder of the presence of God and the rest of the community is indebted to them. These monasteries, convents and retreat houses are places where lay people go for spiritual refreshment. They are invaluable, even though I want to complement them by a theology in which people find God in their ordinary lives, in their relationships, marriage and sexuality. The Second Vatican Council opened the way for the people of God to find him in the physical church and in the domestic church of marriage and family. It also opened the way for people to appreciate their own form of lay spirituality.

Religious life in the past, particularly in convents, offered havens of liberation for women. It is women theologians who are reminding us that, for the overwhelming majority of the Christian period, women were treated as second-class citizens. They were the property of men, violated sexually by them and lacked the opportunity of education. In the convent, women often found their dignity, education and authority. Many an abbess became a leading light in the Church. Today women are discovering their status, authority and dignity in the world at large, and we should rejoice in that. But we must not forget the important role the cloister played in the process of this emancipation. For a long time the cloister was the place that fostered that easy relationship we find in the gospels between Jesus and women.

The world now offers to women the opportunities that the convent offered before. But there will still be women who want to offer their lives in the single state. We need to examine the personality characteristics and the traits that will allow such women to do so and to survive. The key requirement is maturity, an easy term to mention but a difficult one to describe. First of all, the religious life is not for the immature in the sense of those emotionally not ready to face life. Age on entry is important. In the past, it was acceptable to enter religious life and the priesthood in the teens. In the seventies and eighties, when there was an exodus from the religious life and the priesthood, I saw in the course of my work scores of nuns and priests who left. The most common reason was immaturity at age of entry. In those days the Church and the religious life were seen as a source of security. Young men and women unconsciously longed to exchange the security of home for that of religious life and the priesthood. What happened afterwards was simply that, with the passage of time, confidence in the self appeared and some outgrew their need for the secure basis of religious life. The same applies to marriage. People who marry under the age of 20 are much more prone to divorce because, with time, they outgrow their dependent needs on their spouse.

Beyond immaturity, comes difficulties with relationships. Men and women may be shy, finding it difficult to form intimate relationships and so have found attractive the world of isolation that prevailed in religious life. In this world intimacy was taboo. There was a heavy reliance on the vertical relationship with God. Horizontal relationships were frowned upon. Intimacy was not encouraged because, obsessed as we were with the dangers of sexuality, there was a fear of 'special relationships' that suggested homosexuality. Thus, although there was much talk about 'community', there was actually no community, no interaction and particularly no emotional interaction. The lifelong fears of intimacy were sustained, and loving fraternity was absent.

If emotional maturity was absent, sexual awareness was even more frequently neglected. I am absolutely sure that to give up sexuality is a genuine sacrifice that the single person voluntarily offers to God. But the gift he or she offers is the giving up of a reality that is genuine. There is no point in giving up sexuality if one is frightened of it, has not developed sexually, or does not appreciate its meaning or recognise its worth. The single person dedicated to God is as much a sexual person as anyone else, and the true sacrifice is not to offer an absence but a presence that is not genitally actualised. Sexual maturity comes slowly, and it is essential that those who enter religious life should remain open both to emotional and sexual development.

After sexual maturity, the single person dedicated to God must be aware of the problems with authority. Obedience is one of the vows taken by the religious. Obedience is a subtle psychological experience. In childhood our life is dependent on being protected against dangers. We protect ourselves by following the instructions of our parents. Obedience is thus linked with survival. Gradually, we develop our own ability to fend off dangers and we become more self-reliant. With self-reliance comes autonomy. Part of our human dignity is to pay attention to our autonomy.

When an adult is obedient to the authority of a superior, he acknowledges that the superior is there to organise, preserve and secure the life of the community. One of the reasons for obedience is the survival of an organisation, be it a religious community, the army, police and so forth. The ordinary citizen is also expected to obey the laws of the country. Certainly if we did not obey traffic lights there would be carnage on the roads. So obedience in terms of collective survival is self-evident. But obedience in religious life has a further dimension. It is a recognition of authority and ultimately of the authority of Christ. In religious authority, the obedience of Christ to his Father is given as the ultimate example. What is often forgotten is that Christ's obedience was not the blind obedience of a child. It was the response of a commitment out of love. It is not the exchange of a power struggle, with superiority and inferiority at stake.

So obedience in the religious community is not a matter of child-like dependence. The religious person has every right to think for him or herself and to express these thoughts. If they are accepted, all well and good. If they are not, obedience is not a matter of servitude, of a slave to master relationship, but of a commitment of love, as was Jesus' obedience to the Father.

To chastity and obedience, the religious has to add poverty. At the heart of poverty is not a rejection of possessions. Some would say that the kind of life the modern religious lead is a very good one, perhaps even luxurious. The heart of poverty, I repeat, is not possessions. It is the meaning we give to them. Possessions are there to be used and to be admired. What they are not there to do is to give us our sense of identity. As Christians we are not to live by kind permission of our possessions. The kingdom of God, God himself, is the ultimate criterion by which we live.

Chastity, obedience and poverty are not just counsels for the religious. They are, properly understood and maturely exercised, the life of every Christian. Thus the religious, as an ideal, is not a model of impoverishment, sexual and emotional, of obedience and poverty. Ideally the religious is a model of fullness, realised in this life and offered out of love, for prayer and service. In that respect, religious life as a model of fullness offered to God is an ideal that will always remain alive in Christianity.

But how is this to be achieved? In the Church in which I grew up everything was to be achieved by the will. Reason and will were the twin instruments of growth to sanctity and maturity. In addition to reason and will was the belief that deprivation and asceticism were the key to sanctity. Psychology is teaching us that, while reason and will are important, what is more important is to pay attention to what I have described in Chapter 10: the ability to sustain, to heal and to grow. In other words, wholeness or holiness is not to be achieved by deprivation but by incremental accumulation of our humanity. This is not a philosophy of selfishness and self-centredness, but of growth of self-esteem. At the heart of the Christian Gospel is the teaching of loving God and loving our neighbour as ourselves. I believe we cannot give to God or to others what we do not possess. We can do our best with what we possess. At the heart of love is Jesus, who could respond to every invitation because there was nothing he was asked to do which he did not have in the versatility of his personality. He was a rich giver because he had a rich possession of humanity within himself. So, in all my writings, I have turned away from asceticism as the principal means of holiness to personal growth.

How does this growth take place? In childhood we develop physically, cognitively and emotionally. Christians acknowledge these three dimensions of growth, as does everybody else, and so we have food, schooling and the growth of love. There is no doubt that in education Christianity has shown the world what is the best in this field. There is a paradox about emotional growth. The heart of emotional growth is of course love. Love is the central characteristic of Christianity, but Christianity, at least in the Roman Catholic tradition, has chosen to turn to philosophy and reason as its helpmates to understand itself. Even now we have encyclicals on philosophy.[2] In this approach, philosophy is the handmaid of theology. Personally, I have chosen psychology as the handmaid of theology because I believe that psychology has more to teach us about love than any other science.

To physical growth, cognition and emotional development, Christianity adds a spiritual dimension of faith. It is this faith that gives us the ultimate reason for living and loving, and so the home is the place where all the developments take place. In adult life the overwhelming majority of men and women marry and make an adult home where they have their children and the cycle of life continues. In this second home or 'domestic church' that I have outlined, the elements of life can be briefly described in terms of sustaining, healing and growth.

I believe, and many religious who have heard me lecture agree, that sustaining, healing and growth are also essentials of the religious community. In sustaining I have described availability, communication, demonstration of affection, affirmation and resolution of conflict. I have worked with marriage and its problems for 40 years. During this period I have seen scores of men and women in religious life, and nothing that I have learned from this work tells me that these characteristics are not applicable to it. Sustaining, of course, needs intimacy, something that religious communities as they get smaller are finding for themselves. After sustaining, by which I mean surviving physically and emotionally, there comes healing. We are all wounded people, and the nun, priest or monk is no exception. Healing, as I have described before, is an opportunity for us to receive from others a second chance to repair our wounds.

When I first came upon the religious life scene, and nuns were beginning to open up, they often did not know what to do with the wounded in their midst. I joked that when a Mother Superior found such a person difficult, not knowing what to do, she sent that person off on course after course to get some peace. Religious communities are now beginning to realise that they must not accept the very wounded with whom they cannot cope. A religious community, which is truly loving, is an ideal place for healing. This requires intimacy, openness, the ability to listen and to listen endlessly to the stress of others. Listening means that interpersonal communication is just as important as a vertical relationship with God. Through interpersonal intimacy we give each other experiences that we have failed to obtain as children, such as affirmation, acceptance, confidence, encouragement, personal meaning, significance and ultimately unconditional acceptance. In this confidence, self-esteem returns.

Beyond sustaining and healing comes growth, by which I mean emotional growth. Emotional growth involves a shift from dependence to independence. Dependence essentially is the relying on others for our survival.

Independence is the ability to make up our own minds, to trust and rely on our own judgements, and to cope with our aloneness. Finally, from independence we move to interdependence, the hallmark of community life. Emotional growth implies recognising our anger. It used to be thought that anger had no place in Christian life. Jesus himself was angry on more than one occasion. Psychology has taught us that anger can be healthy and that conflict can be a source of growth. Anger has to be recognised, expressed reasonably and appropriately, and added to forgiveness and reconciliation. Forgiveness and reconciliation must recognise that anger has its reasons, and part of the follow-through of anger is to remedy its causes. Emotional growth also implies sexual growth. This means the recognition that we are all sexual persons, that the erotic attracts the single person as much as anyone else, and that as single people we fall in love and can give expression to that love without genital involvement. Jesus loved many people and he could be close to women, whom he admired, without physical involvement.

In addition, in the life of the religious there is a spiritual dimension, that is the life of liturgy, worship and prayer, which is of outstanding importance, but there are dangers. The first is the establishing of a vertical relationship with God at the expense of a horizontal relationship of love with our neighbour. There is a danger of centring and focusing on spirituality as a way to understand love. The kingdom of God is humanity at the service of God. The religious have to understand their essence, not only in terms of liturgy, worship and prayer, but also as developing human beings who offer themselves in the service of love. They need to sharpen their humanity as much as their spirituality.

The single person dedicated to service is offered as an example of the reality that there will be no marriage in heaven. Jesus makes it clear that there will be no marriage in heaven, but that does not mean that there will not be intimate relationships of love there. The very idea of heaven as currently understood is an intimate relationship with God. There will not be procreation, but the energy of love will undoubtedly contain a powerful erotic element, for the erotic is a nexus or network of attraction that is at the root of loving communication. Thus erotic love exists among single people but is not consummated genitally. So, while the religious do not marry, they exhibit loving relationships within which, as sexual beings, they are influenced by erotic attraction.

What about the spiritual status of the single person dedicated to God? Though the Council of Trent emphasised very strongly the dignity of sacramental marriage, it condemned those who maintained that the married state was preferable to that of virginity or celibacy. It also condemned those who maintained that it is not better or more blessed to continue in the state of virginity or celibacy than to enter into the state of matrimony. This view of the single state was influenced by centuries of pessimism about sexuality that has only started to die out in recent times. The Church needs time to reconsider the significance of marriage and sexuality.

There is no point in debating in the abstract which is the higher state. The unifying factor is the degree of availability in love. There are, I am sure, millions who, in their married loving availability, live truly saintly lives. Their absence from the list of canonised saints is a genuine blot in the book of Christianity. There is no justification whatsoever for the bias of canonisation towards single people. That does not mean that the married are superior to the single. I suspect that comparing one state to another is a dubious exercise. As a fulfilled married man of nearly 50 years of marriage, I can look with admiration at the religious and priests I have met in my life. I have no doubt that, temporarily, while we are proclaiming the value, dignity and worth of sexuality, there might appear to be a diminution of religious vocations, but I am certain that this is a temporary hurdle. As men and women accept sexual maturity in their lives, the vocation of loving availability, which is the essence of the single state, will reassert itself.

Religious communities have a distinct advantage over the single celibate priest working in the parish. Community is the model of the Trinity. It is the model of persons in relationships of love, and that is the essential nature of being a Christian. Isolation, asexuality and loneliness are distortions of being human, hence the last chapter. But in so far as religious life is a community of love, it is an authentic presence of God, where its members can sustain, heal and grow as persons whose loving availability is at the service of God.

From what I have written in this chapter it can be seen that I believe the absence of the genital expression of sexuality is no handicap to a mature and healthy life. I write this because the opposite view is held with no justification. Freud was aware of this and referred to it as sublimation. What is essential in life is love, not genital sex. However, whilst genital sex is not essential, it is very important as an expression of love. Love remains the key and we are beginning to realise this. In 1998, Dr D. Ornish[3] systematically outlined the subtle interaction between the lack of stress, worry and the positive presence of loving intimacy, and the immune system. Love actually protects the person.

It is not the sexual philanderer but the committed lover who is the supreme example of mature humanity and, in Christian terms, the saint. In so far as the single person dedicated to God lives in a community of love, which encourages the growth of love, available for the service of God, then indeed the single life is an authentic presence of God. This is what I understand by Jesus' declaration in favour of eunuchs for the kingdom of God, men and women full of love who dedicate themselves to make this love available for the kingdom of God. In this respect I shall do all I can in my work and writings to foster their presence. Although we live at a time of some reduction in their numbers, I am sure that the call to this life is part of a genuine voice of Christianity.

In the midst of a book devoted to the goodness of sexuality as an authentic human and divine gift, I want to proclaim repeatedly that love comes before genitality. Those who proclaim it fully are the secular lovers and Christian saints. There is no contradiction in this book.

This chapter has been primarily concerned with the single state dedicated to God, but there is a whole range of single people not in that state: the widows, the divorced, the single mother, the unmarried for one reason or another, people in transition, people with normal personalities and people with interpersonal difficulties. As single people, they all need love and affection. They often find these in friendship. So what is the link between friendship and sexuality? Single people are sexual people. This statement needs expansion. In our ordinary understanding of sex, we take it for granted that we mean genital sex, but this is not the only human sexuality.

From the time of Freud and his successors, we have come to realise that libido or sexual energy resides in our bodies as sensual capacities, which we express physically through touch, hugs, kisses and caresses. Thus a combination of friendship – as understood in this book and elsewhere in my writings as the forces of sustaining, healing and growth, coupled with physical expressions of sexuality through human contact – involves the life of the single person in a combination of friendship and sex through intimacy. Friendship has been seriously undervalued in Christianity, which has emphasised marriage or the single state dedicated to God. However, relationships of friendship within the single population have their own dignity and sustaining power.

Given the context of this book, it is appropriate to say at the end of this chapter, indeed to repeat what I have said before, that, some people at some time in their life, temporarily or permanently, do not have access to satisfactory sexual relations or indeed to sexual relations at all. Are they less than fully human?

It is clear that, from the time of Freud, sexuality is an intrinsic part of our humanity. Its expression in sexual intercourse is the realisation of an essential human characteristic. This book extols this fact, which was diminished for hundreds of years in the Christian community, and I insist that its absence is a loss. However, I would say two things. Firstly, sexuality is intimately linked with love, and the presence of love is a powerful compensating factor for the absence of sexual intercourse. Secondly, the human personality derives its meaning also from other sources. The body with its sensations has its own significance. The mind with its cognitive abilities has its own rewards, and for many, intellectual achievements have a prominence of place. The heart with its feelings and emotions also gives rich rewards.

All this is not to say that, although sexual intercourse has a prominent place in human experience and the fulfilment of the human personality, it is indispensable. There is plenty of evidence that one can be truly human in its temporary or permanent absence.

Chapter 23

Theology

In the course of nearly 40 years working and writing as a psychiatrist with a special interest in marriage and sexuality, I have often received letters attacking me for a particular position I expressed. In my replies, there is insufficient space to offer a comprehensive response. I take an opportunity in this chapter to offer a justification of my position. Most people who criticise me begin by asking the fundamental question: by what authority I presume to teach? Let me say at once that I do not presume to teach. Moral teaching in the Catholic Church is the responsibility of the Pope and the bishops in consultation with the people of God. I am absolutely clear about this and have no wish to change one iota of it. Having said that, we are only at the beginning of the story. The Vatican II Constitution on the Church defined it as follows: 'By her relationship with Christ, the Church is a kind of sacrament or sign of intimate union with God, and of the unity of all mankind. She is also an instrument for the achievement of such union and unity.' Father Kelly,[1] to whom I owe a lot in writing this chapter, goes on to say, 'Of course, this definition of the Church applies to the whole people of God. Hence, its application should not be seen as principally, and certainly not solely applied to the Church precisely as institution. As Avery Dulles has pointed out, the church as institution is only one model of the Church and it has a very limited validity. It is the whole church precisely as the people of God who have a special competence in the area of wise and loving living.'

As a psychiatrist, I am conscious of the danger of power. I am very wary of the contemporary attention paid to authority and power in the Church. In company with many other people, I find the centralisation of power in Rome not a healthy sign. I understand the fear of the Pope of losing the grip of power in case the Church fragments, but I believe at present it is too centralised. The model suggested by Vatican II of the Pope, in his supreme Petrine office, working in conjunction with the bishops and the bishops in turn with priests and lay people, is a much more fitting, mature model. I am conscious of the danger of central activity, behaving as a parental figure, treating the members of the Church as children. Concerned as I am for evangelisation, I think this model is another cause for a large exodus from the Church. The people of God have outgrown their dependence on authority and want to be taken seriously as adults. This movement was beginning to take place at Vatican II, but it has been officially sidelined. In the light of the growth of the maturity of the people of God, I am certain we must go back to the vision of Vatican II.

Following this general outline but still in the sphere of authority, I am sometimes accused of wanting to usurp the power of the teaching Church. This is a recurrent implication that I want to be Pope. My critics cannot expect to know my motivation for my writings and so, in a typical psychological way, project on to me hunger for power and its usurpation. On the contrary, my motives for my writings are the desire to make the Church credible and strong, for the world needs more than ever an authoritative teaching voice. The world, however, is not easily duped. When the Church teaches, it must be sure that it really knows what it is talking about. It has divine assistance in this teaching, but nevertheless it needs authentic knowledge to guide it. It must be an informed Church and not a biased one. In being informed, two things are needed. The first is authentic information, and the second is an unbiased selection.

It goes without saying that to acknowledge and respect the teaching authority of the Pope and the bishops is non-negotiable. It goes without saying that this teaching carries a presumption that it reflects Christian truth. When it comes to the handling of sexuality by the Catholic Church, we must be wary of a tradition that has given many false trails. These are a handling of the truth by primarily celibate men, with all the bias of inherent patriarchy, absence of sexual experience and ultimately the personal biases of the teacher. This does not mean that the Church is incapable of teaching truth.

Consider the wonder of the teaching of Vatican II on marriage and sexuality. Nevertheless, all its teaching on sexuality and marriage has to be carefully evaluated by Christian principles. In the selection of teaching, the personal biases of the person matters, hence it is vital that the selection is made independent of the bias of the personality. But that is not always possible and mistakes will be made. When the suggestion is made that the Church can make mistakes, for some the most acute anxiety is generated. This anxiety is translated into attacking those who challenge the teaching. I understand this reaction very well psychologically.

Absolute faith in the teaching of the Church becomes part of the very identity of some people. Any change in teaching is ultimately a threat to their very being. Those who go round proclaiming a stout defence of the Pope and attacking anyone who disagrees, are, despite all appearances, not concerned so much with the Pope, but with their own survival. They have made papal authority the very basis of their security and of their faith. For biases do exist at the very heart of the teaching tradition. One of these biases in my opinion is clinging to the link between procreation and sexuality that undermines *Humanae Vitae*, not that procreation is unimportant. It is that the teaching does not reflect accurately its meaning in depth.

Everyone recognises that for the Church to teach authentically on marriage and sexuality, it needs the assistance of married people. I quote from the late Cardinal Hume's intervention at the 1983 *Synod on the Family*: 'The prophetic mission of husbands and wives is based upon their experience as married persons and on an understanding of the sacrament of marriage of which they can speak with their own authority. This experience and this understanding constitute, I would suggest, an outline source of theology from which we, the pastors, and indeed the whole Church can draw.' My writings stem from nearly 50 years of happy marriage, four daughters and the insights of the psychological and psychiatric training I possess. The *Instruction to Moral Theologians*, which Father Kelly deals with in detail, states that there is a need for 'a solid and correct understanding of ourselves as human beings, of our world and of God. To acclaim this the instruction recognises that the human sciences have an indispensable role to play. They help us to delve more deeply into the truth about ourselves as bodily, sexual, interdependent, social, cultural and historical beings.' This invitation by the Church to make a contribution as a social scientist, referred to extensively in the Vatican II Council and since, is one that I have taken very seriously and have responded to in over 20 books. This does not mean that all my contributions reflect the truth. As a scientist, I am accustomed to peer review and criticism. What happens if my insights lead me to challenge official teaching?

This is what lies at the heart of many letters I receive. Put in a simplistic way, they are saying, 'How dare I disagree?' Karl Rahner, the eminent theologian, said in 1964 something that is still important in our day: 'It (Executive authority in the Church) must keep alive the consciousness that it is a duty and not a gracious condescension when it accepts suggestions from "below", that it must not from the start pull all the strings, and that the higher and in fact charismatic wisdom can sometimes be with the subordinate, and that the charismatic wisdom of office may consist in not sheltering itself from such higher wisdom.'[2] It is clear from this passage and many others that the Church has a duty to listen. But what happens when there is disagreement between the prevailing teaching or view and those offered from 'below'?

The *Instruction to Moral Theologians*, quoted by Father Kelly, brings out the points which the instruction wishes moral theologians to take note of. I am no moral theologian and have never made a claim to be so. I remain a lay person with special expertise in the subject of marriage and sexuality. Nevertheless, I find the points raised by the *Instruction* are relevant wherever disagreement exists. The first point the *Instruction* makes is for the 'tendency to regard a judgement as having all the more validity to the extent it proceeds from the individual relying upon his own powers', and so, 'freedom of thought comes to oppose the authority of tradition which is considered a cause of servitude'. The attitude the *Instruction* condemns as 'dissent' believes that 'a teaching handed on and generally received is *a priori* suspect and its truth contested' and that 'freedom of judgement is more important than the truth itself'. As far as I am concerned, and in so far as I understand the *Instruction*, it is saying that dissent consists of making freedom of judgement more important than truth itself. This is a philosophical position I do not hold. I have never believed that I should be fighting for freedom of thought. I believe freedom of thought is important, but only as a source of illuminating Christian truth.

Next the *Instruction* makes the point in which it describes dissent as an attitude that claims 'a kind of "parallel Magisterium" and that some people are setting up a supreme Magisterium of conscience in opposition of the Magisterium of the Church'. As far as I am concerned, I have offered my views as only opinions to be considered. I have never made a claim to Magisterial authority. There can only be one Magisterium in the Church. My concern is that what it teaches and does enlists the consent of the people of God and other Christians. My main interest is that what is taught and practised should not undermine the authority and integrity of the Church. I can say with utter conviction that what I have written in this book has been expressed in previous books and in widespread lecturing around the world. It corresponds largely with the views of other Churches and meets a wide consensus.

Still continuing with dissent, the *Instruction* says, 'in its most radical form (dissent), aims at changing the Church following a model of protest which takes its inspiration from political society. More frequently, it is asserted that the theologian is not bound to adhere to any Magisterial teaching unless it is infallible. Doctrines proposed without exercise of the charisma of infallibility are said to have no obligatory character about them, leaving the individual completely at liberty to adhere to them or not. The theologian would accordingly be totally free to raise doubts or reject the non infallible teaching of the Magisterium, particularly in the case of specific moral norms.' In this respect I would like to assert that I have never protested in a style that derives its inspiration from political society. I am opposed to all forms of coercion. I prefer to approach my differences by writing that deepens the truth.

The *Instruction* is afraid that non-infallible teaching will be taken as open to easier change, and in fact the Vatican has increasingly tightened the conditions for accepting its teaching as binding. Here my only point would be that I do not believe that truth becomes persuasive by surrounding it with more and more authority. Truth is at its best when it persuades by what it contains. I am not saying that Christian truth should be subject to scientific criteria of proving its authenticity. Christian truth is wider than scientific objectivity. All I am saying is that it is not desirable to persuade through creeping infallibility because people simply rebel.

Father Kelly goes on to say that, while there is no question of forming a parallel Magisterium, there remains the situation that, after serious reflection, a theologian might find him or herself in disagreement with an individual item of teaching. Then disagreement is the only appropriate response he or she can give to that teaching. The overwhelming majority of the contents of this book are non-controversial. Some are suggestions for change, which many consider appropriate, such as the marriage of priests. It is only in the case of *Humanae Vitae* that there is direct disagreement. I have stated that I do not consider myself a moral theologian. So how do I see myself in the Catholic Church? I can do no better than quote Vatican II: 'For this the Church was founded, that by spreading the kingdom of Christ everywhere for the glory of God the Father she might bring all men to share in Christ's saving redemption; and that through them, the whole world might in actual fact be brought into relationship with him. All activity of the Mystical Body directed to the attainment of this goal is called the apostolate and the Church carries it on in various ways through all her members . . . In the Church there is a diversity of service but unity of purpose. Christ conferred on the Apostles and their successor the duty of teaching, sanctifying and ruling in his name and power. But the laity, too, share in the priestly, prophetic and royal office of Christ and therefore have their own role to play in the mission of the whole People of God in the Church and in the world' (Degree of the Apostolate of the Laity II).

I take these words very seriously and throughout my life I have worked for the good of this apostolate by writing, lecturing and advancing knowledge in the field of my competence. My dedication to Christ is absolute and as I wrote in my recent book,[3] all my life I have felt a special love for him. In so far as the Church really reflects Christ, it elicits the same love. In so far as it acts as an institution of power, mimicking the world, I am unhappy. I see the Church as a community of love and throughout its history it has flirted with worldly power far too much for my liking. Nevertheless, though I do not claim to be a moral theologian, as an ordinary layman with special responsibilities, I have to follow a code of Christian life in what I do. My critics would really like me to keep silent, obey and leave all the thinking to the Curia. In my opinion this would be an abandonment of my responsibility. I see it as a fantasy of those who do not want to be disturbed and want peace of mind at any price. Given that my conscience demands that I write what I see to be the Christian truth, nevertheless I impose upon myself a certain discipline. I see this discipline as first of all being well informed about the topics I write about. My writing is no mere wish fulfilment. It is subject to rigorous scientific probing, as well documented as possible and allied to the authentic teaching of the Church. I never disagree before I give the teaching of the Church. I take seriously the view that anyone reading my material should be as well instructed in what the Church says as in what I say. The aim is an informed conscience and in this respect I am one with the mind of the Church.

Next I deal psychologically with my inner world. I believe anger has a place in the human personality as much as the desired assent of the will to the teaching authority. I am aware that there are a lot of hurt people in the Church as a direct result of its teaching on marriage and sexuality. I hasten to add that I am personally not one of these hurt people walking in anger. Although I find *Humanae Vitae* unacceptable, in my own marriage we used only birth regulation methods acceptable to the Church. But I meet people who are hurt and angry. The official answer is that this hurt is the result of obeying Christ. In some cases it may be so, but I am clear in others that it is not and that, with the best intention in the world, the Church inflicts unnecessary wounds. Given that many people are hurt and angry, what can we do with this anger?

I believe that some have taken their anger out by leaving the Church and leaving their orders, and rebel in ways that are unacceptable. While I understand and have much sympathy with their feelings, I do not agree with their actions. It is clear that some of the ways that the Church deals with its theologians is not right, and the late Cardinal Hume voiced his anxieties in these matters in his address to the American bishops. Many have voiced concern about the way that justice is not seen to be carried out in dealings with theologians. I do not know the case for both sides. We only hear the shouts of those who feel unjustly treated. I am sure that the Church is not an intrinsically unjust institution, but situations arise when concern occurs.

In all these situations, I return to the matter of anger. My experience as a psychiatrist tells me that it is possible to forget the reason for anger and to pursue anger in its own right. I think that amongst those who are rebelling, there are those who pursue anger for its own sake. In my own life and motivation I have studiously avoided falling into this trap. In the course of my work I see many Catholics who are hurt over their broken marriages, contraception (less and less), homosexuality and other sexual problems. I feel angry on their behalf, but the answer is to love them and to love the Church that could do better. In my writing, I aim to persuade the Church by the evidence I present, not by my destructive anger.

But some of my critics would say that I am destroying the Church by seeking to change it. In this respect, Father Kelly writes, 'I get the impression that some Catholics today are haunted by a feeling of fear, suspicion and insecurity. It is almost as though they are afraid to trust the movement of the Holy Spirit within the Church. They see no place for real dialogue within the Church ... It is too threatening since it suggests that the Church is also a learning community which has to be open to change.' These men and women are frightened of change. They live in a bliss of ignorance of the history of the Church: they are probably unaware of the monumental changes that Vatican II achieved in the teaching of marriage and sexuality. If anyone wants to be persuaded of what change guided by the Holy Spirit can do, they have only to look at what was achieved at the Second Vatican Council. Despite the retrograde steps that have since taken place, the base of the Catholic Church was changed at the Council. Sooner or later we shall return to resume where we left off.

Change in the official teaching is threatening because it is believed it undermines the faith. It is believed that if the Church can change in one area, how can we believe in the rest of its teaching? This view rests on the attitude that truth is contained in that which does not change. The truth is the teaching of the Church under the inspiration of the Holy Spirit. The truth never stands still, and those who are aware of the changes in marriage and sexuality will appreciate that the evolved truth of the Council expressed Christian vision much more completely. So I am sure that if and when the teaching of *Humanae Vitae* changes, then the Holy Spirit will ensure that Christ will be revealed even more completely.

So I conclude with my motivation for writing this book. I start by saying that all I am doing is offering ideas and opinions. I am not offering an unarguable case that the Church must accept. The people of God are invited to peruse its contents. I have studiously avoided elementary errors of theology, but there might be some and no doubt they will be brought to my attention. Any caring criticism is more than welcome.

Chapter 24

Evangelisation

For a great deal of Christian history, sexuality was seen as the work of the devil and as promoting his kingdom. In this chapter I shall reverse things and look upon sexuality as a means of evangelisation.

I begin by looking at a fact which is startling, and yet is ignored by the remnant which remains Christian, namely the massive withdrawal of people of all ages, particularly the young, from church attendance. I do not document this phenomenon in figures, of which there are plenty, but rather I appeal to what everybody knows is a reality. Yet the governing bodies of all the Churches go on as if nothing of significance is happening. They look inwards, attending to the needs of an ever-shrinking remnant, arguing about abstract subjects, issuing encyclicals of little relevance to evangelisation and discouraging any attempt at forward-looking inspiration. At the end of the twentieth century, conservative forces in all the Churches are presiding over the presence of Christianity as we know it and are looking to the past for solutions. People in some Protestant quarters are turning to fundamentalism and others in the Roman Catholic Church look back to a golden past. As far as the latter is concerned, in the last 20 years it has stifled the voice and vision of the Second Vatican Council and is pursuing a policy of maintenance of an ever-shrinking worshipping community. There is no strategy of reclaiming the people of God. Those who see the emptying of the pews are crying out for an inspiration, are desperate for a vision of the Second Vatican Council to be restated and for the Church to engage with the world. The Second Vatican Council was set up to deal with a crisis. The crisis continues and the vision of the Council is dimmed.

Secular society is in the throes of materialism and science. We have to respond to materialism by appreciating that happiness is not to be found in the depths of material goods. While the minimum of material goods is necessary, there is a point where accumulation becomes a disease. There is a teaching in psychology that proclaims the value of the 'good enough' – good enough mothering, good enough care, good enough attention – rather than the seeking of perfection. Good enough material availability is the answer to greed and material selfishness. The 'good enough' of the lay person is the equivalent of the vow of poverty of the religious. What it says is that human identity is not derived from the amount of possessions owned but from the inner world of the person.

We have to respond to science by embracing it. My professional world is that of psychology and psychiatry and, in the 40 years that I have studied and practised, it has illuminated my faith more than anything else. Christianity has been afraid of the social sciences. Indeed, it has turned back to what it knows, namely philosophy, which has assent from the highest authority. There is nothing wrong with philosophy, except that its subject engages the truth in an abstract form, while the social sciences and medicine engage in the immediacy of living.

Beyond materialism and science that affect all Christian Churches, there are the wounds that the Churches have inflicted on themselves. I can only speak about the Roman Catholic Church which I know personally. Its wounds are many, but I shall refer to only two of them. First of all, there is its reliance on authority. The pre-Vatican II Church relied on authority and fear to bring people to church. People came to church to 'get mass', to 'hear mass', to fulfil an obligation, to obey a rule. Transgression of the rule was what mattered, not love of Christ. The fact is that the relationship between parent and child, which was the link between the Magisterium and the people of God, has receded because the people of God have grown up. The attempts to reimpose this authority are doomed, because that age has gone. This is what I mean by the Church's failure to have a strategy for evangelisation. It is trying to return to a conservative, authoritarian past. This approach appeals by and large to those who, while adult, remain children at heart and want authority to govern them. But most people have grown up and are voting with their feet by keeping away from church. Yet the Second Vatican Council showed the way by promoting a partnership between the Pope and bishops, bishops and the people of God. There is no alternative, and sooner or later we must return to what the Holy Spirit proclaimed.

From what I have said in this book, it is now clear that sexuality is an essential aspect of the human personality. In other words, in its presence, we are reflecting one of the succinct aspects of the image of God in us. Although the image is certainly expressed in the miracle of procreation, its most powerful link is with human love. Two thousand years of linking sex with lust and sin have distorted our vision of sexuality as reflecting one of the most powerful experiences of the presence of God.

If what I am saying is remotely true, then Christianity has the capacity to teach the people of God that in the experience of sexual attraction, the erotic and sexual intercourse is to be found a profound presence of the reality of God. I am not suggesting, as some will hasten to accuse me, that we worship sexuality, but rather that we celebrate its presence and appreciate in it the existence of God. In particular, we appreciate sexuality as a powerful component of love which is the essence of God. For me, one of the great impoverishments of Christianity is that we connect God with love at every turn, but that we do not acknowledge the occasions we experience sexual love as God-appointed moments. Think of what it would do for evangelisation, particularly of the young, if we connected their sexual attraction, erotic feelings and sexual intercourse with the presence of God.

Staying with the presence of God in everyday life, I want to move from the young to the married. The Church has been sensitive enough to recognise that one of its glories is to see marriage as a sacrament. Part of my ecumenical hopes is that the reformed churches will also see the sacramentality of marriage. The Second Vatican Council recognised marriage and the family as the domestic church. It is the furthest it has gone to see the Church as a worshipping community of the people of God outside the parochial church. It is a marvellous concept and tallies very much with my idea of finding God in everyday life. In the domestic church there is, as I have described, the liturgy of the married in their every moment of relationship, culminating in sexual intercourse when they enter the very heart of the Trinity. Through sexual intercourse, they enter a recurrent act of love through which the love of God joins their human experience of love. As embodied people, they live the very centrality of the incarnation in the love of their bodies. They have the miracle of procreation and sexual intercourse as the nurturing experiences for the love and education of their children.

For me, God is found in the domestic church, brought to the parochial church on Sundays and celebrated there in the mass. In turn the God of the Word and the Eucharist is brought back into the home. The domestic church was a precious idea of the Second Vatican Council. In the interval it has sunk without trace. I have no illusions that the ideas outlined in this book for evangelisation will not face formidable obstacles, and yet I am concerned that we have to face the reality of people not coming to church.

Every age has the challenge of promoting the realisation of the presence of God. Two thousand years have formulated the reality of God in prayers, sacraments and liturgy. No one would claim that these are all exhaustive. If we go back to the gospels, we find Jesus using food, healing and love as three powerful means of demonstrating the kingdom of God. It is no surprise that I want to extend love in terms of sexuality. In case any one misinterprets what I am writing as an attack on the parochial church, clergy, sacraments and liturgy, let me say at once that nothing is further from my mind. What I am saying is that, as practised at present, this combination is preventing millions of people from worshipping God. I am asking whether God is not inviting us to look more widely. This is not to say that I have not used the parochial church to celebrate sex and marriage and to link them with God. For many years now, at the end of our parish pre-marriage course, we have a liturgical celebration in church in which lay people and the priest present an outline of love and sexuality using the Scriptures as a background. We invite the whole parish, and many people come and appreciate the link between God and their human experience.

I am really focusing on the general concept of linking human experience with God as part of evangelisation. We do this with the sense of morality, but I want to move on from the sense of right and wrong to celebrate our embodiment, relationship and love.

A whole book could be written about evangelisation in terms of celebrating God in our everyday experiences and then bringing them to the altar of the church, thus linking our physical and emotional realities with God. I intend to write such a book, but in this chapter I have outlined some of its features.

Chapter 25

Morality at a Time of Sexual Revolution

The twentieth century saw an unprecedented change in our vision of sexuality. The combined efforts of Sigmund Freud (1856–1939), Theodore Hendrick van der Velde (1873–1937), Havelock Ellis (1859–1939), Alfred Charles Kinsey (1894–1956) and Masters and Johnson in our day have changed our understanding of sexuality. Freud showed that it was an essential component of the human personality. The others measured it and taught us to accept sexual pleasure as something good and desirable. There can be no doubt that this was a great trauma for Christianity. In the space of a hundred years, the work of these people undid what was put in place in the first five centuries of the Christian era. It has to be said that the Christian community has found it hard-going to absorb all the implications.

There are two areas in which the shock has been most severe. The first is the displacement of procreation as the primary purpose of sexual intercourse. This has resulted both from the work of the above pioneers and as a result of social changes. Marriage lasts much longer than it did and sexual intercourse continues into the sixties, seventies and even later. The size of the family has been greatly reduced, leaving procreation an unnecessary element for the overwhelming majority of sexual acts. To facilitate this, contraception has become widespread, with all the Christian Churches accepting it, apart from the official Roman Catholic Church.

The second area is sexual pleasure. For 2,000 years sexual pleasure has been regarded with suspicion and embarrassment and, as

Luther thought, marriage was seen as a remedy for the human wounds of concupiscence. The work of researchers has allowed us to embrace sexual pleasure with open arms. This frightened Christians, who feared that such a step would lead to unbridled sexual behaviour. In effect, as has been shown in this book, nothing of the sort has happened. The overwhelming majority of sexual acts take place within the context of an ongoing, enduring, committed and faithful sexual relationship. Promiscuity has not become rampant. There is certainly more and earlier sexual activity outside traditional marriage but, as already stated, cohabitation, which is the alternative form within which the majority of sexual intercourse occurs, safeguards the major needs of sexual acts. Not only has promiscuity not become widespread, but the freeing of sexual pleasure from inhibition has allowed Christianity to reclaim some of its own traditions, such as the Song of Songs. It has also allowed men and women to rejoice and discover this extraordinary divine gift.

But the transformation has not been without trauma, argument and debate.

Conservative circles are apprehensive about the changes. They put the worst interpretation on facts and figures, look to a golden past to reverse the present tide of change and fear the dissolution of the family. There are two particular platforms in the conservative response. The first for many Protestants is a biblical one. For such an approach the Bible is a short-cut solution to every problem. It is forgotten that the roots of biblical teaching are a combination of inspired writing set within a social period with its own customs. The teaching on adultery and fornication in the Old Testament reflects the status of woman as an inferior being, within a patriarchal framework in which she was seen as the property of the man. Patriarchy was widely influential at the time of both the Old and the New Testaments, and some of the Pauline teaching on women would be completely unacceptable today. Fundamentalist views on sex do not do justice to the primary criterion of New Testament teaching, namely that everything human has love as the basis of its integrity.

The moral teaching of the Roman Catholic Church is based on a combination of tradition, natural law and the Scriptures. In the Second Vatican Council, the Catholic Church made a giant step forward in its teaching. The changes were monumental and are still not really appreciated by Roman Catholics. I quote from *New Directions in Sexual Ethics* by Father Kevin Kelly,[1] who summarised the changes in the Council:

1. They adopt a new vocabulary for speaking about marriage, preferring to speak of marriage in terms of covenant or relationship than in the language of contract.
2. They drop the terminology of 'primary and secondary ends of marriage', preferring a more 'personalist' approach to marriage, even defining marriage as a relationship in which the couple 'mutually bestow and accept each other'. (This is the language I have tried to explain in this book.)
3. Faithful married love has its source in God's love and when expressed in 'mutual self-bestowal' is caught up in divine love. By implication, therefore, the expression and deepening of this love by sexual intercourse is also 'caught up into divine love', something which many Christian writers down the centuries would have found it difficult to accept. (This is a particular point I have tried to develop in this book.)
4. The lifelong character of marriage is based principally on the nature of the couple's loving relationship rather than on the needs of the children.
5. Children are the supreme gift of the love relationship rather than the primary end of marriage.
6. Limiting the size of their families can be a responsible (even at times necessary) decision for Christian couples.
7. Not being able to express their love sexually for each other can be harmful to a couple's marriage. Where the intimacy of married life is broken off, it is not rare for its faithfulness to be imperilled and its quality of fruitfulness ruined.
8. There is nothing wrong in a married couple making love even when their intention is not to have children, since that maintains 'the faithful exercise of love and the full intimacy of their lives'. The actual 'means' of birth regulation adopted are to be judged ethically and not simply in the light of the couple's intention, but according to 'objective criteria', based on the 'nature of the person and the person's acts'. (In this respect I hope this book advances

our understanding of the nature of the person and the person's acts.)

The last paragraph of the Council's teaching, which was followed by the encyclical *Humanae Vitae* that forbade contraception, has become a source of great controversy within the Roman Catholic Church. This matter has been considered in Chapter 20. It is sufficient to say here that the controversy has done a great deal of harm to the further advancing of the magnificent work of the Council. Moral theologians and lay people have been frightened to court the disapproval of the teaching authority of the Church and so, with notable exceptions, they have kept silent about the whole subject of sexuality. This is not a book about authority and the Church, but about the meaning of sexual intercourse.

In my view, the sexual revolution is one of the most monumental changes in civilisation with enormous implications for evangelisation. It is not a question of who is right and who is wrong about contraception. It is a question of putting contraception within the wider perspective of the meaning of sexual intercourse and giving young people an understanding that Christianity reflects the glory of this divine gift. So ultimately the Roman Catholic Church must battle with its conscience to get the teaching right. There is tension and I personally know how many are afraid to speak out in case disapproval descends upon them. A small minority believe the Church has got it right, the large majority believe it has got it wrong. My own position has been clear for some time, but I believe that it is vital to get the wider picture of sexuality right. Hence I have written this book which examines sexual intercourse in the light of personal love, carrying on where the Second Vatican Council left off.

One of the important transfigurations in Christianity today is that more and more the Churches are thinking ecumenically and, in his book, Father Kelly describes this dialogue in Chapter 5. What he has to say is most illuminating. The Churches are trying to catch up with the sexual revolution. From a wider angle, what the Churches teach is described in Stuart and Thatcher's *People of Passion*,[2] and for an excellent summary of the present position of Christianity, particularly that of the Roman Catholic Church, reference should be made to Gareth Moore's article in the book *Sex, Sexuality and Relationship.*[3]

In the meantime, the tension and the debate continue. Whatever is written about the morality of cohabitation or contraception, and in the wider field of sexual ethics about masturbation, remarriage of the divorced and homosexuality – subjects which are not considered in this book – there will be men and women who find themselves outside the present norms of Christian teaching. What should the attitude of the Church be to these men and women?

There are those who want to apply the rigorism of the law and the Bible. There are many and various reasons for their stance. Biblical fundamentalists see violations of the Bible as unacceptable. Roman Catholics cannot, in the matter of contraception, accept that the Church can err and for some, who are totally ignorant of the sexual issues, obedience is the only thing that matters. My reply is that every age has its complex moral issues and what matters is the pursuit of truth. One of the greatest challenges of our age is sexuality and getting our attitude right about the subject is more than a matter of the teaching of the Magisterium. It is a question of getting the divine plan of sexuality right, and this is an urgent matter for evangelisation. I believe that one of the reasons for the mass alienation from Christianity is its perceived view on sexuality. This must be corrected.

Changing views takes time. In the meantime millions cohabit, millions divorce and remarry, millions of Roman Catholics use contraception and so on. How do we approach these men and women? As I said, there are those who favour the rigorism of the law either as seen in the Bible or in canon law. Law and punishment, including exclusion from the sacraments, is one response. Is it the response Jesus would give if he were here? His response was to speak about the kingdom of God, to clarify what the kingdom requires and to support those who are on a journey to realise that kingdom. This support is not about punishment and exclusion, but about forgiveness, compassion and inclusiveness in the Christian community.

At a time of unprecedented change, we have to do two things: first we have to explore the truth about sexuality. This we must do with the help of the social sciences and compare what they have to teach us with tradition and Scripture, which sometimes may need to be reinterpreted. This has to be done carefully. The whole history of Christianity is about an evolving understanding of truth as it reflects divine reality. Sexuality is no exception. The secular society has opened many possibilities but it has also, in some respects, trivialised sexuality. We must welcome the genuine and evaluate it by the principles of love that remain the only Christian criterion of assessing the truth. Secondly, there are many sexually wounded people and they seek our love. We cannot offer rigidity or the law. There is only one Christian response and that is compassion and love.

The Church is a community of love, and Jesus came to seek those who were not in good health. Whenever we have to respond pastorally to an individual, we have to say not what the law dictates but what Jesus would have said. We do not have Jesus to answer the question. Some Roman Catholics will say we have the Church, which relies on tradition, natural law and the Scriptures. We know that tradition and natural law have laid false trails in the field of sexuality. While the Church is ultimately the source of truth, it takes time for the truth to unfold.

In the meantime we can get things in perspective. Those who believe that there is sexual moral chaos in contemporary society are wrong. They derive their view from a fantasy world of films, fiction and the media. In reality, detailed research shows that the overwhelming amount of sexual intercourse takes place within established relationships that reflect either marriage, cohabitation or exclusive relationships. What should cause much more concern is marital breakdown with its devastating effects on the couple and their children. The sexual revolution has undoubtedly produced changes, but there is no moral chaos as far as sexual intercourse is concerned. There is much more quantitative continuity with the past in the presence of enormous qualitative change for the better.

Chapter 26

Assessing the Sexual Revolution

Readers will have noticed that Christianity has come a long way from where the early fathers placed sexuality. The shift has taken place literally in the last 30 years which, in historic terms, is a short time. Nevertheless the behaviour of people, and particularly the young, has undergone a revolution to which the Churches must respond. I am really only familiar with the Roman Catholic Church and I am well aware that this Church, despite the amazing progress it made at the Second Vatican Council, is stuck. There are some people who believe that the only thing at issue is a matter of loyalty and obedience, finding sufficient humility to accept the teaching of the Magisterium. There are others, myself included, who are convinced that the Church is haemorrhaging, and that one of the reasons is sexuality. Belonging to the second group, I have to make an assessment of the sexual revolution. Is it a singular gift to mankind or is it a mixed blessing? I remember in my youth and later, a Church obsessed with sexual sin, manuals that guarded people against transgression from everything from fornication to masturbation, and the pews of the confessional filled with people confessing sexual sins. The erotic was approached with apprehension, and marriage was seen as a state that legitimised sexual intercourse, but did not celebrate it. Sexual intercourse was tied to procreation, not to love. All this offered a massive negativity to the precious gift of sexuality. Although this affected primarily the Roman Catholic Church, other Churches also suffered. It was as if Christianity was adamant to say that, 'In the beginning was the word and the word was "No".'

I still see in my work men and women who were damaged by this phase of Christianity, and so the only thing that can be said is that such an era must never return. I am not sure if the Magisterium appreciates what enormous damage it inflicted on the people of God. I rejoice to see an era of sexual liberation and the opportunity for Christianity to appreciate this divine gift.

Although Christianity has its own internal resources to have made the change, there is no doubt that the sexual revolution is a secular event just as celibacy is a specific concern for the Christian community.

The sexual revolution started in the nineteenth century and flourished in the twentieth. The work of Freud, Havelock Ellis, Kinsey, Masters and Johnson and others have taught us to recognise that sexuality is not an added factor, but an essential characteristic of our personality. We are sexual, embodied beings. This should not come as a surprise to Christians who believe that the Son of God took flesh. This embodiment of the Son of God has yet to find the fullness of its glory.

The widespread extension of contraception freed women from the fear of pregnancy and liberated them to rejoice in sexual pleasure as had been the experience of men from time immemorial. We have become aware through feminism of the insidious grip that patriarchy has over sexuality and the injustices perpetrated by men towards women. Double standards in sexual behaviour are giving way to a more egalitarian enjoyment of sex.

Kinsey, who, although criticised, has never been radically challenged, revealed how widespread premarital sexual intercourse and adultery were at an age where orthodoxy would have liked to believe that Christian standards prevailed. Kinsey not only revealed the incidence of premarital and extramarital sexual intercourse, but also uncovered the hidden incidence of homosexual and other minority sexual practices. The hidden and the guilt-producing surfaced for all to see. By bringing the underworld of sexual behaviour to the surface, talking, discussing and exchanging views, hypocrisy has receded. Society as a whole became aware of the depths of the range of sexuality. Men and women were liberated to own their sexuality. This ownership of sexuality has still some way to go, because in sex men and women encounter a mystery and this mystery elicits awe. If sex elicits awe, fear has also been reduced.

With the recession of fear, sexual minorities, homosexuals, bisexuals, transvestites and others have emerged to claim their rightful place in society. We still have some way to go to accept unconditionally these men and women, but they have found champions both from within and outside their circle to claim their rights. Where fear, hypocrisy, guilt, shame and embarrassment once prevailed, men and women can now begin to acknowledge their sexuality without getting rattled.

All this is a massive step forward in a civilisation which can now lay claim to the goodness of the erotic and of sexual intercourse. But is all this undiluted progress? In my opinion it is not. For while the twentieth century has gone a long way to liberate sex, it has also trivialised it. It has done this in a number of ways. First of all, the discoveries of incidence by Kinsey and the work on sexual intercourse by Masters and Johnson emphasised heavily the biological. Certainly the work of Masters and Johnson has allowed many therapeutic advances that are invaluable. The result of the sexual liberation has left society with a technology of sex, without an adequate link to love and sacredness. Sacredness is not a prerogative of Christianity. It is an inherent human characteristic. Sex is allied to life, new life and the growth of love. The emphasis on biology has detracted from wholeness and holiness.

In the wake of the sexual revolution, we are left with the pursuit of the orgasm. However important the orgasm is, this is only a scientific measurement of sexual success. Both men and women, but particularly the latter, appreciate the orgasm, but they prefer to set sexual intercourse in an atmosphere of love. There is no major writer or researcher on sex who has made a comprehensive investigation of the emotional loving side of sexual intercourse. I am not saying that what I have written in this book about the meaning of sexual intercourse is the whole or even a partial answer. But no one would deny that sexual intercourse has a personal dimension. In our schools, 50 years of sexual education have advanced biology at the expense of love. The advance of the orgasm as the climax of sexual activity has given rise to an atmosphere peddled by the media that the amount of sex realised is what matters, and not its quality. In practice, as I have often referred to in this book, the majority of sex takes place within loving relationships but that is despite the revolution, not through its efforts. The revolution has favoured the impersonal. The media are free to celebrate fantasy. In television programme after television programme, the forbidden, the scandalous and the erotically exciting are pictured as the pinnacle of human aspiration. A particular bone of contention of mine is that the media portrays repeatedly the falling in love stage and says little about the contribution of sexual intercourse to the maintenance of relationships.

In the balance between showing the importance of the sexual minorities and marriage, the sexual minorities are given much more attention. Marriage is treated by the media as old-fashioned, stale, stifling and oppressive. It is clear that some of these criticisms are accurate. What is forgotten is that marriage and the family are vital for health, happiness, the realisation of love, the upbringing of children and the centre for imparting love from generation to generation.

In this context, marriage is a platform for life and we, as yet, have found no alternative to it. On behalf of life, great advances have been made with the care of pregnancy, premature babies and obstetric difficulties. This is good as indeed are the advances that have been made to help women become pregnant. Against these pro-life advances, it must be said that the consequence of sexual intercourse in terms of life itself have not received a similar boost. I am against abortion, but I am even more against abortion on the trivial social reasons for which it is allowed. The sexual revolution has done no favours to the unborn child.

What the sexual revolution has achieved through medicine, at least in the West, is the considerable defeat of sexually transmitted diseases. These have not been entirely eradicated, but they have been controlled. Amongst the insensitive who extol casual sex, the presence of such diseases are camouflaged by the use of antibiotics, but antibiotics are no substitute for love in a personal relationship.

The absence of love in the portrayal of sexual intercourse is also to be found in the greatly enlarged pornographic literature. Hard and soft pornography have multiplied, as one of the objects of the sexual revolution is to encourage sex to the point of orgasm by any means. Sexual titillation and impersonality are the hallmarks of pornography and they have certainly increased.

185

In brief, the sexual revolution has confronted the world and Western society in particular with a vital part of being human. To that extent it is a success. In so far as it has distorted and trivialised the sexual identity of men and women, it has dehumanised us.

What should the Christian response to the sexual revolution be? In so far as the twentieth century brought mankind nearer to an appreciation of the divine gift of sex, Christianity should embrace the revolution. This embrace should not be a 'dragging of feet' affair. The Churches should recognise a gift when offered one. We should be grateful to the sexual pioneers but we should also be critical. The Churches have a difficult task here. Their tradition does not exactly make them welcome champions who are heard on sexual matters. The media tend to emphasise their hostility to homosexuality, abortion, any unjust harsh treatment of women and so on. They do not shout about the proclamation of the goodness of the Churches speaking about the gift of sex. But that is precisely what we need to do.

Just as the Middle Ages married Aristotle with their theology, so Christianity has to marry the sexual revolution with revelation. It has no alternative. If in the Catholic Church celibate men and women find it difficult to understand and appreciate the details of sex, they need to listen to their fellow Churches and the married amongst their own people. What we must not do is to procrastinate. Life is moving fast and the young who need to integrate their sexuality with their faith, have not got much patience. So Christianity must be positive about this gift of sexuality. Some steps have already been taken to move in that direction.

In the past the Churches have emphasised respect for life. That tradition is good and must be maintained. The tendency was to emphasise the biology of life. The real gift that Christianity has to offer is to link sexuality with love and life. Love is a word that is heard from the pulpits of all the Churches, Sunday after Sunday. It is a word with a broad meaning that cannot easily be pinned down. The branch of science with which I am familiar, namely psychology, is making great contributions to the understanding of love. I have incorporated as much as I understand of it in this book, but there is a lot more to be done in this area.

In speaking of sex with love, Christianity will be responding to what is missing in the sexual revolution and what people instinctively want to hear. But it must overcome our reticence. All the Churches and the Roman Catholic Church in particular have a habit of looking to the past for their direction and inspiration, and so they should for revelation is their springboard. The Roman Catholic Church in addition pays great attention to tradition, but Christianity needs to forget and bury a great deal of its sexual tradition. This makes things difficult, but it managed to do so in the Second Vatican Council and the other Churches have also moved forward.

As far as revelation is concerned, we have the Song of Songs and other scriptural writings that denote the goodness of the erotic and sex. Let us reclaim them. In the gospels we have the incarnation of Jesus as the epitome of the sacredness of embodiment, his treatment of everything human in terms of love and the supremacies of beings in community of sexual love as the symbol of the Trinity. We are not short of material from revelation and we can retain what is best in tradition.

Christianity must embrace sexuality and critically assess it in terms of love. This criticism must be done with care and not out of the rejection of sex. The world expects Christianity to reject sex, but we must not fall into that trap. Sex is good and holy but everything the sexual revolution has achieved is not necessarily good. Christianity must act as a friendly critic.

Its first task is to educate its own people. Even if this book is found wanting in many respects, there is a major message in it that needs to be heard. How often do we hear from the pulpit a positive sermon about sexuality? We need an 'Amen' to sexuality. It is 'Amen' to our humanity, and we must not compartmentalise our humanity to body and soul. Dualism has played havoc in Christianity and it has no place at its centre. We are whole people, a unity of body, mind and heart, and we are people of passion. For 2,000 years Christianity tried to beat that passion out of existence. It never succeeded wholly, but it managed to put a cloud over sexual pleasure, the erotic and sexual intercourse. The sexual revolution put passion back on the agenda and Christianity must embrace it. Passion is not without its dangers and Jesus knew this when he warned against the look of lust. It is only too easy to mistake passion for lust. The Christian answer in the past was to suppress sexuality.

The genuine Christian answer is to welcome it and to welcome it so much that we can distinguish between loving passion and using the human person as an object of lust. We must choose person and not lust, not out of fear but because we are educated to select love.

Hence my attention to sexual education and the detailed examination I have given it. Some will say that I have not prohibited enough, that I have caved in to the indulgence of the times and have rehabilitated cohabitation. My answer is what are we going to do with the millions who cohabit? Are we going to issue a proclamation excommunicating them all and banning them from Church attendance? Are we going to refuse to marry them? I have tried to introduce the concept of accepting sexual pleasure and the erotic as a legitimate authentic experience, as in the Song of Songs. The extended period between puberty and marriage should be a sexual celebration of love. Given their traditions, all the Churches find some difficulty in this.

When sexual intercourse takes place in the context of an ongoing, enduring, committed, exclusive and faithful relationship, its integrity is safeguarded. I have not written about sex among the elderly, but I have hinted that sexual intercourse continues after the menopause for several decades. The exclusive link between sex and procreation made no sense of sex after the menopause. Sex in terms of initiating and facilitating relationships of love makes sense of sex at any time.

Ultimately, we have to make sense of sex in the context of what Jesus said, i.e. that there will be no marriage in heaven. For those who see sex exclusively in terms of marriage, this is the end of sex. When sex is seen primarily as the principal force of love that maintains relationships, then we are right at the very heart of the life of God and the Trinity.

At the conclusion of this chapter, what is the balance sheet for the sexual revolution? It is a major event that cannot be ignored, and it has penetrated and percolated all our lives. To ignore it is to ignore a major component of life. It has transformed the way we see ourselves. Christianity must embrace it and rejoice over it. But it must perfect it by introducing a large dose of its own specific dimension, that is love. When Christianity speaks about love it speaks about what makes all human beings tick. The conjunction of sex and love is the Christian answer to the revolution. Having said that I do not want to omit the fact that Christianity has received from Jesus a specific revelation about the single state dedicated to God. While it must embrace sexual love, it must also proclaim the single state.

I finish by repeating what I have said before. In my opinion the sexual revolution is a major challenge to Christianity that can either be denied or embraced with Christian wisdom and revelation. I believe that such Christian transformation finds itself in the word love, which is the essence of God, and so the main point of this book is to marry sexuality with love. Secondly, I am seriously disturbed by the haemorrhaging from the Church of people and its priests. I think one of the reasons for this is sexuality, and this book is a small contribution to a strategy for evangelisation. Thirdly and finally, in all my work I strive that through service and my writings the face of Christ should be illuminated and seen more clearly. To sum up, the aim of the book is love, Christ and the Church, but above all the manifestation of Christ as love in the world.

References

Chapter 1

1. John Paul II (1994), *The Theology of the Body*, London, Daughters of St Paul.
2. Countryman, L. W. (1988), *Dirt, Greed and Sex*, Philadelphia, Fortress Press.
3. Douglas, M. (1966), *Purity and Danger: Analysis of Concepts of Pollution and Taboo*, London, Routledge and Kegan Paul.
4. Dominian, J. (1998), *One Like Us: A psychological interpretation of Jesus*, London, Darton, Longman and Todd.

Chapter 2

1. Brown, P. (1988), *The Body and Society*, London, Faber and Faber.
2. Soranus, *Gynaecia* 17.39.2, Ilberg.
3. Council of Elvira, *Canon 33*, Jonkers ed.
4. Power, K. (1995), *Veiled Desire*, London, Darton, Longman and Todd; Noonan Jnr, J. T. (1986), *Contraception*, Harvard, Harvard University Press. See also Brown, *The Body and Society, op. cit.*
5. *Casti Connubii 1930*, London, CTS.
6. Augustine, *Confessions*, 8.7.17: 757.

Chapter 3

1. Gregory I, Epist XI, LXIV, in a letter to Augustine of Canterbury, Resp. ad. die. interrog.
2. Noonan Jnr, J. T. (1986), *Contraception*, Harvard, Harvard University Press.
3. *Summa Theologica III Suppl.*, 9.41, art. 3, ad 6.
4. Messenger, E. C. (1948), *The Mystery of Sex and Marriage*, part 2, London, Sands.
5. *Summa Theologica III*, 9.41, art. 3, ad 2.
6. Dominian, J. (1967), *Christian Marriage*, London, Darton, Longman and Todd.
7. De Sales, F. (1962), *Introduction to the Devout Life*, London, Burns and Oates.

References

Chapter 4
1. D T C, 9.2225, cf De Captivit Babylon, Cap de Matrimonio.
2. Porter, M. (1986), *Sex, Marriage and the Church*, Victoria, Australia, Dove.
3. Luther, *Hochzeitpredigt on Heb XIII*, C. Werke (e) III.
4. Luther cf *Grosse Katechismus*, C. Werke (e) XXI.
5. Calvin, In Epist I ad Cor, n VIII, 6, opera VII.
6. Baily, D. S. (1959), *The Man-Woman Relationship in Christian Thought*, London, Longmans.

Chapter 5
1. Brecher, E. M. (1970), *The Sex Researchers*, London, Andre Deutsch.
2. Kelly, K. T. (1998), *New Directions in Sexual Ethics*, London, Chapman.
3. Hoose, B. (1998), *Christian Ethics*, London, Cassell.
4. Stuart, E. and Thatcher, A. (1997), *People of Passion*, London, Mowbray.
5. The Lambeth Conference 1930, Resolution 15.
6. Doms, H. (1939), *The Meaning of Marriage*, London, Sheed and Ward.
7. Dominian, J. (1967), *Christian Marriage*, London, Darton, Longman and Todd.
8. The Lambeth Conference 1958, London, SPCK and Seabury Press.
9. (1978), *Marriage and the Church's Task*, London, CIO Publishing.
10. Report of Commission on Human Sexuality (1990), Methodist Publishing House.
11. Human Sexuality 1994 in the Church of Scotland Reports to the General Assembly, Peterborough.

Chapter 6
1. Stoller, R. (1969), *Sex and Gender*, London, Hogarth.
2. Diamond, M. 'A critical evaluation of the ontogeny of human sexual behaviour', *Quarterly Review of Biology*, **40**,147.
3. Bancroft, J. (1995), *Human Sexuality and its Problems*, Edinburgh, Churchill Livingstone.
4. Galenson, B. A. and Roiple, H. (1974), 'The emergence of genital awareness during the second year of life', in R. C. Friedman et al (eds), *Sex Differences in Behaviour*, New York, Wiley.
5. Kinsey, A. S., Pomeroy, W. B. and Martin C. F. (1948), *Sexual Behaviour in the Human Male*, Philadelphia, Sanders.
6. Dominian, J. (1998), *One Like Us: A psychological interpretation of Jesus*, London, Darton, Longman and Todd.
7. Shaver, P., Hazen, C. and Bradshaw, D. (1988), 'Love as attachment', in R. J. Sternberg and M. L. Barnes (eds), *The Psychology of Love*, New Haven, Yale University Press.

References

Chapter 7
1. Dornbusch, S. et al (1981), 'Sexual development, age and dating', *Child Development*.
2. Schoof-Tams, K. et al (1976), 'Differentiation of sexual morality between 11 and 16 years', *Archives of Sexual Behaviour*, **5**.333.
3. Udry, J. R. et al (1985), 'Serum androgenic hormone motivates sexual behaviour in adolescent boys', *Fertility and Sterility*, **43**.90.
4. Wellings, K. et al (1994), *Sexual Behaviour in Britain*, London, Penguin.
5. *Teenage Pregnancy*, (1999), London, Social Exclusion Unit.

Chapter 8
1. Sullivan, S. (1999), *Falling in Love*, London, Macmillan.
2. Masters, W. H. and Johnson, V. E. (1966), *Human Sexual Response*, London, Churchill Livingstone.
3. John Paul II (1994), *The Theology of the Body*, London, Daughters of St Paul.
4. Moore, G. (1992), *The Body in Context*, London, SCM.

Chapter 10
1. Dominian, J. (1981), *Marriage, Faith and Love*, London, Darton, Longman and Todd; Dominian, J. (1987), *Sexual Integrity*, London, Darton, Longman and Todd; Dominian, J. (1991), *Passionate and Compassionate Love*, London, Darton, Longman and Todd.

Chapter 11
1. Documents of the Second Vatican Council (1967), *The Church Today*, 50.

Chapter 12
1. Dominian, J. (1968), *Martial Breakdown*, London, Pelican Books.
2. Dominian, J. (1984), *Make or Break*, London, SPCK.
3. Bancroft, J. (1983), *Human Sexuality and its Problems*, Edinburgh, Churchill Livingstone.

Chapter 13
1. Dominian, J. (1988), *Sexual Integrity*, London, Darton, Longman and Todd.
2. Thatcher, A. (1999), *Marriage after Modernity*, Sheffield, Sheffield Academic Press.

Chapter 14
1. Wellings, K. et al, *Sexual Behaviour in Britain*, London, Penguin.
2. *Teenage Pregnancy* (1999), London, Social Exclusion Unit.

References

Chapter 15
1. Moore, G. (1998), *Sex, Sexuality and Relationships in Christian Ethics*, London, Cassell.
2. Population Trends, Summer 1999, Office of National Statistics, London.
3. Thatcher, A. (1999), *Marriage after Modernity*, Sheffield, Sheffield Academic Press.
4. Kiernan, K. (1999), *Cohabitation in Western Europe*, Population Trends.

Chapter 16
1. Wellings, K. et al (1994), *Sexual Behaviour in Britain*, London, Penguin.
2. Lawson, A. (1988), *Adultery*, Oxford, Blackwell.
3. Gorer, G. (1971), *Sex and Marriage in England Today*, London, Nelson.
4. Blumstein, P. and Schwartz, P. (1983), *American Couples*, New York, Morrow.
5. Dominian, J. (1995), *Marriage*, London, Cedar.

Chapter 18
1. Dominian, J. (1998), *One Like Us: A psychological interpretation of Jesus*, London, Darton, Longman and Todd.

Chapter 20
1. Noonan, J. T. (1986), *Contraception*, Harvard, Harvard University Press.
2. Kinsey, A. C. et al (1948), *Sexual Behaviour in the Human Male*, London and Philadelphia, Sanders.
3. Second Vatican Council, *Declaration on the Laity*, chap IV.37

Chapter 21
1. Kerkhofs, J. (1995), *Europe without Priests*, London, SCM Press.
2. Porter, M. (1996), *Sex, Marriage and the Church*, Victoria, Australia, Dove.
3. Sipe, A. W. R. (1990), *A Secret World*, New York, Brunner/Mazel.
4. Kelly, K. T. (1998), *New Directions in Sexual Ethics*, London and Washington, Chapman; Stuart, E. and Thatcher, A. (1997), *People of Passion*, London, Mowbray.

Chapter 22
1. Dominian, J. (1998), *One Like Us: A psychological interpretation of Jesus*, London, Darton, Longman and Todd.
2. Pope John Paul II, *Fides et Ration*.
3. Ornish, D. (1998), *Love and Survival*, London, Vermillion.

Chapter 23
1. Kelly, K. T. (1992), *New Directions in Moral Theology*, London, Chapman.
2. Rahner, K. (1964), *The Dynamic Element in Church*, London, Burns and Oates.

3. Dominian, J. (1998), *One Like Us: A psychological interpretation of Jesus*, London, Darton, Longman and Todd.

Chapter 25
1. Kelly, T. K. (1998), *New Directions in Sexual Ethics*, London, Chapman.
2. Stuart, E. and Thatcher, A. (1997), *People of Passion*, London, Mowbray.
3. Moore, G. (1998), 'Sex, sexuality and relationship' in B. Hoose, *Introduction to Christian Ethics*, London, Cassell.

Index

Index